NO
HE
CAN'T

NO HE CAN'T

HOW **BARACK OBAMA**
IS DISMANTLING HOPE AND CHANGE

KEVIN MCCULLOUGH

THOMAS NELSON
Since 1798

NASHVILLE   DALLAS   MEXICO CITY   RIO DE JANEIRO

Published in Nashville, Tennessee, by Thomas Nelson. Thomas Nelson is a trademark of Thomas Nelson, Inc.

Thomas Nelson, Inc., titles may be purchased in bulk for educational, business, fund-raising, or sales promotional use. For information, please e-mail SpecialMarkets@ThomasNelson.com.

Scripture quotations marked ESV are taken from THE ENGLISH STANDARD VERSION. © 2001 by Crossway Bibles, a division of Good News Publishers.

Page design by Mandi Cofer

Library of Congress Cataloging-in-Publication Data

McCullough, Kevin.
  No he can't : how Barack Obama is dismantling hope and change / Kevin McCullough.
    p. cm.
  Includes bibliographical references and index.
  ISBN 978-1-59555-338-6 (alk. paper)
  1. United States—Politics and government—2009– 2. United States—Economic policy—2009– 3. Obama, Barack. I. Title.
  E907.M34 2011
  973.932092—dc22

                              2011000087

Printed in the United States of America

11 12 13 14 15 16 QGF 6 5 4 3 2 1

Dedicated to Rosemond and James, with a pledge to do all that is within my power to raise you where clarity is in abundance and thinking to excess is greatly encouraged.

Contents

Contents

Contents

Foreword

By Mike Huckabee

I can't tell you how *wrong* I wish Kevin McCullough had been in 2006.

I know that's an odd way to endorse a book, its author, and its general purpose, but that was the feeling I had about his prediction in December 2006, when he became the first pundit to predict the eventual rise and electoral success of the first-term senator from Illinois to the White House.

A man named Barack Obama.

With prescient clarity, though, Kevin nailed the circumstances, the place in history, and what he saw nearly two full years before the election played out to near-perfect precision.

Kevin saw a perfect storm on the horizon at that time that didn't just add up to Democrats taking control of the White House. It also added up to a new kind of Democrat that was aided by the fatigue of two wars, an economy at that time that was just beginning to unravel, racial tensions long ignored in the American election cycle, and the co-opting of evangelical Christians, so much so that 4 out of 10 of them would vote for a man whose position on vital issues to their faith stood in steadfast opposition.

Kevin even nailed the combination of nominees that would change what could have been one of the closest elections of our lifetime to an electoral blowout with several traditionally red states flipping to blue.

Kevin predicted that three candidates in particular would make

Obama's win even easier. He went so far as to imply that if a former mayor of New York, a new "convert" to conservatism—who had written a very early blueprint to "Obamacare" for his state's health care reform—or a U.S. senator known as "the Maverick" were to successfully vie for and land the nomination, Senator Obama would sail to victory. (I was really grateful he didn't list any former governors from Arkansas.)

Yet those things that Kevin saw long in advance of everyone else added up to the exact formula that took President Obama to the White House, and an attempted "fundamental transformation of America" was under way.

The day after his syndicated column was published on Townhall .com, Rush Limbaugh, the most-listened-to voice in politics in America, read Kevin's prescient piece almost word for word on his daily radio show. Limbaugh's reaction wasn't dissimilar to several others among day-to-day politicos and bean counters. At the time Limbaugh, like most of the nation, didn't know much about Obama, but you could tell by the fascination in his voice that what he was reading made sense.

The one key element between Kevin McCullough, Rush Limbaugh, and Mike Huckabee at the time was this: we all hoped Kevin was wrong.

The piece he had written was written more as a warning and a dire plea to the electorate to make a different decision from what appeared to be coming into place.

Kevin had me on his talk show throughout the 2007–2008 electoral season. My campaign was sorely short of the kind of cash that flowed into other candidates' secret PACs that sometimes were used for nefarious purposes in attempting to slander other candidates.

It was in that cycle that I began to get a sense of who Kevin McCullough is; how much he loves his God, his family, and his nation; and what great burden lay on his heart at seeing what was headed for our future—because he had seen it so far in advance.

Since 2008 Kevin and I have spent some time together on more than just a few occasions. In the process I've had a chance to chat about numerous things with him. And one observation I've taken away from those conversations is something very important: he cares more about the idea of *clarity* than any person I've ever met.

He wishes to cut through the double-speak of Washington, so that everyday people—folks of all sorts who are working hard to pay their bills and raise their kids—aren't harmed by government's innate desire to grow bigger.

He wishes to sort out the truth from the untruth in ways that empower the people who engage their culture, their families, and their nation.

He wishes to be as transparent as possible, so that those who read his columns and books, those who listen to his talk-radio entities, and those who watch his morning television broadcast understand that he is owned by no one and nothing except his convictions.

Sometimes, even in an interview with presidential candidates, he is willing to annoy those he is interviewing, so that those who are *listening* learn the things that are truly important in the process.

I will disclose that Kevin has often expressed his support for my positions on the issues, and like many others has offered his thoughts on my own future. He's even offered up a new prediction on presidential politics, one that includes another Huckabee run for the White House. I have neither confirmed nor denied the possibility, though to listen to Kevin's assessment gives you pause for thought, especially given the rationale he used to so accurately predict the 2008 outcome.

The book you hold in your hand is important because of the no-nonsense, honest, and straightforward approach Kevin uses to dissect four significant areas of the Obama administration's failures. In the areas of the economy, national security, values we believe in, and ultimately, accountability to "We the People," Kevin has assessed—and I believe quite accurately—why "Hope and Change" did not turn into the "fundamental transformation" that most voters believed they were going to receive.

But what I genuinely love about this book is that he doesn't end the story with what went wrong, but at the end of most of the chapters adds "a bit of clarity" as to how America can and needs to right the ship. In some ways this text is one of the most genuinely hope-filled books to espouse common-sense conservative ideas in quite some time.

Kevin is also one of the fairest pundits in America today. He is not a partisan; he votes his conscience, and he is able to point out flaws, but also admit success.

What follows is not a text designed to stir up hate or anger. It is instead a passionate defense of what America needs, and has not received, from an administration that promised so much.

No one will ever confuse Kevin with someone who does not have an opinion. But I am also glad to say that his opinions never prevent him from being a decent human being to his fellow man.

At least this has been my experience, and I gather it will be yours as well, once you've read the book you hold.

Ideas matter, words have meanings, clarity always trumps unity, and Kevin McCullough illustrates these principles clearly in the pages ahead.

If you find yourself in the midst of some of the debates of the day, buy a couple of copies of this book, and give to friends, read them together, discuss the larger principles involved, and see for yourself if you don't end up coming to the same conclusions. I think your brain will be better for the journey!

All the best,

Gov. Mike Huckabee
Host, *Huckabee*, Fox News

Introduction
Shadowing the Community Organizer

My professional life is entangled with that of a man I've never met.

At the beginning, it all felt so random, but in retrospect it almost seems like divine providence. There was a strange sort of inevitability about how each event fell into place as I feared—as I *knew*—it would. I chose to remain silent until the facts presented themselves, and was then reluctantly dragged into the debate on the side of his opposition. It was a role that I accepted, but not one I eagerly embraced.

No, from that time until this, I have shared a path with the forty-fourth president of the United States of America that I never hoped for and never wanted. Yet at this moment, because of the great crises facing our nation, battered and scarred as she is with economic, national security, and moral challenges, I must speak.

FACING THE REAL DEFICIT

At the time of this writing there are many wounded, hurting, and suffering families in America. There are many more worldwide. Unemployment is roughly 10 percent across the nation. Prices for everything from food to gasoline to housing—in fact, everything we pay for—are on the rise, even as the value of our currency declines. Bailout programs have failed. The record stimulus package performed so poorly that the politicians—better skilled at self-protection than simple observation and learning—are busy discussing another. The average family is making less, working harder, and stressing more now under the current administration than at any single point under the previous.

War continues on two battlefronts. Gitmo is still open for business. A commander-in-chief who once pledged to bring home the troops "and to bring them home now" has instead increased deployments. Without, it should be added, a commensurate increase in support. As a result, emotional distress, bankruptcy, divorce, and even suicide attempts are at all-time highs among America's fighting men and women. Despite all the proposed spending, somehow our government has not found a way to keep the most basic of promises to those returning from the front, defending our freedoms, curbing tyranny and terrorism, and putting smiles on the faces of Iraqis and Afghans with new schools, safe neighborhoods, and improved infrastructure.

And if our economic and national security concerns are not significant enough to speak genuinely and honestly about the impact of the current administration's policies, then certainly the erosion of our God-given rights is. Today we see good constantly and almost systematically confused with evil. We see indecency first labeled as tolerable, then appropriate, and finally preferable. We see the core beliefs of our founding documents shredded in the grist mill of the power drunk and the arrogant. We see that a man's word is worth as little as yesterday's mail. We see a president's adviser whisper words of exploitation in his ear, counseling him to leverage his people's pain to advance his agenda.

This is not the change for which America signed up—to say nothing of the hope that was supposedly in the bargain.

Some claim this has all been a premeditated bait and switch. Others say that the current situation is born of well-intentioned, if mistaken, policies. Whatever the case, one thing is clear: regardless of the causes, the United States is now facing one of the greatest crises of her history. A deficit of staggering proportions has formed, a huge, gaping sinkhole of a deficit. I am not talking about the deficit of dollars or trade. The deficit we are so sorely and woefully short on is one of the most valuable commodities of all time. If it could be traded as currency, America would heal herself overnight.

We are in a deficit of common sense.

I've been peddling common sense for the better part of a decade, primarily through the mediums of published text, syndicated columns, and nationally syndicated talk radio. I have also spent a good deal of time in the theater of life. Life in Chicago, Illinois, to be specific, and that's where my path would intersect with Barack Obama's for the first time. Obama's arrival to the city of Chicago in 1985 preceded my own by only four years. He came as a community organizer and was nine years older than me. I was a still-wet-behind-the-ears theology/journalism student. We would leave Chicago within only months of each other, he for the U.S. Senate and I for the next step in the world of talk radio.

His labor on the city's south side seemed worlds away from my college campus downtown. Yet, as the years passed and as his ambitions grew (it was during his community organization days that he first ran a failed attempt for a higher office before finally settling into his place in the Illinois state legislature), the writing on the wall became so clear to me that early on I labeled him as "one of the most dangerous politicians our generation will see."

I did so not because he was evil personified—I don't believe him to be. Though in my syndicated writings, I have labeled many of his policies as such. I labeled him "dangerous" because of his effectiveness, his smoothness of tongue, his Kennedy-like quality of looking like a starting point guard who also dates the captain of the cheer squad. He had it all: connections with the powerful black clergy of Chicago's South Side, the doting wife, beautiful babies, and a smile that could sell three billion boxes of Wheaties.

Although that may not sound like a description of a dangerous person, I believe it's not the aura of a man that measures his threat, but his determination, his substance, and his network. With Barack Obama, that truism came with a glossy coat of "All-American."

At times that was the stab that hurt the most.

OBAMA VOTES TO LET BORN CHILDREN DIE

One of those times was when—as a member of the state legislature of Illinois—he insisted that the members take up the debate over whether a hospital operated by Obama's own denomination should outlaw the procedure of allowing newborn disabled children to die of starvation and neglect right there in the pediatric wing.

Believing that his future runs at office might be dependent upon the support of certain women's groups, it was important for Obama not to allow himself to be seen as "weak" on any issue that remotely resembled the question of abortion. Thus, his record on abortion-related issues had to be seen as unmovable.

Counter to the vast majority of Americans, Obama moved to the most extreme ground possible, threw down the stake, and claimed the territory. He advocated not merely for the morning-after pill, the use of RU-486, early trimester elective abortion, second-trimester elective abortion, abortions without parental consent, abortions without parental notification, the placement of abortion clinics on school grounds, or even transporting minors across state lines to gain access to abortions not provided in their home state, but he then broke new territory.

Obama supported late-term abortions, also properly referred to as *partial-birth abortions*. But even that was not enough.

When the issue was brought to a vote of whether or not unwanted disabled children who had been born despite abortion procedures should be allowed to die from starvation, neglect, and lack of medical care, Barack Obama became the only federally elected officeholder to have ever voted in favor of allowing those children to die. It was on that day that I realized

Obama, a big-grinning, shoot-some-hoops kind of guy from Chicago's South Side, was also a ruthless pragmatist.

If there had been another way that he possibly could have held the endorsement of Planned Parenthood for his U.S. Senate race, perhaps he would not have cast the vote to let born children starve, but the fact that he did spoke volumes about what he would sacrifice to get where he needed to go.

ROCKETING FROM SPRINGFIELD TO WASHINGTON, D.C.

When the time came, and he declared his intention for the Senate seat held then by U.S. senator Peter Fitzgerald, Illinois was in a state of political shock. Scandals rocked the government statewide, governors were going to prison, and corrupt Democrats were cheating the system and rigging the vote. Inept state office holders only made things worse, and federal officeholders from the state were asked to "play the heavy" on the wrong side of many issues. With such incompetence on the Republican side, it was no wonder Senator Fitzgerald, who had been perhaps the lone voice of sanity in the state for some time, wished to no longer serve. It would soon be only a matter of time until Dennis Hastert was gone, Judy Baar Topinka had "blown up" (and out), and Henry Hyde had passed away.

In this environment it was a blast to do talk radio in Chicago. Never a city to be outshined by others when it came to political corruption, Chicago rose to new infamy. Rudy Giuliani was cleaning up New York City, Los Angeles had not yet seen its current-day challenges, but the "combine" was alive and well in the Windy City. The "combine" was a cacophony of state Democrats and Republicans striking under-the-table deals, creating oppressive state and local government, and going to jail together in the process.

In the throes of the wide-open 2004 election cycle, plenty of people wanted to grab a piece of the U.S. Senate race pie. So with a half dozen

Republican candidates, and nearly twice that in the Democratic ranks, I expected to be up late on primary night to see who the eventual representatives would be.

The Republican voters chose the charismatic Jack Ryan. A young man who had taught at an inner-city school, Ryan had also made gobs of money on Wall Street and married a Hollywood model and actress. When it appeared that he still hadn't found meaning in anything else, he sought to make a difference in the next generation.

The Democrats chose a charismatic young man for themselves as well: Barack Obama.

In the days that followed, Ryan's campaign flamed out due to the savvy, behind-the-scenes, cutthroat strategies of the Obama camp. The Republicans brought in Alan Keyes as a carpetbagger, for reasons many still scratch their heads at, and Obama more or less floated his way to Washington, D.C., and right into the U.S. Senate.

But what observant people saw in that election trend was shocking. Obama had not been the favorite among all the primary candidates, yet he walked away with the nomination on election night, gathering more votes in the collar counties (traditionally more Republican counties) and in the City of Chicago itself—a place where he had never held a single office, than all the rest of the candidates of both parties. Combined!

At the time I was doing daily talk radio for a 50,000-watt AM station with my gracious cohost, Deborah Rowe, whom I still count as a very good friend. Deb is African-American and resided on the South Side, and later in the south suburbs. We shared an office and a penchant for debate. On the topic of whether or not Obama would run for president in 2008, I never wavered from my belief that he would. She claimed he would not know enough by then and that it would be too soon for him to make the attempt.

Fewer than two hundred days into his first and only term as U.S. senator, Barack Obama checked my box on the "I told you so" scoreboard. By that time, I had been promoted to a bigger radio station in New York

City. There I was doing daily talk radio in the only city in America that was more racially diverse than Chicago, and even more opinionated.

During Obama's campaign for Senate, I began to tell the New York audiences my impressions about Obama as a man, but more important, as a strategist. In Barack Obama there were two people, I frequently told them. It was easy to see if they would just picture the charm of a Bill Clinton and the ruthless strategy of a Hillary Clinton. People were intrigued but way too busy at the time to count my little analogy of much importance.

THE AUDACITY OF WINSOMENESS

Then, in the fall of 2006, something quite disturbing took place. Pastor Rick Warren, author of *The Purpose Driven Life*, invited Barack Obama (who had not yet officially entered the 2008 presidential race, but had formed his exploratory committee and had begun fund-raising) to speak at his church. With Warren's invitation to address his congregation from behind the pulpit, in the auditorium where his normal Sunday services took place, he offered Obama something that no one else in America could: an audience of Christians he could snooker.

As I wrote my syndicated column in advance of the event, I stated firmly my belief that Obama was using Warren to gain an audience and an implied acceptance from the evangelical community. I even went so far as to predict that he would later point to that appearance as an implied endorsement of sorts. I firmly believed it did not matter what Rick Warren's intentions were in the matter, but that it was the intentions of the ruthless charmer that needed to be considered. In a matter of days, through my column, then my radio show, and then external media pings, tens of thousands of phone calls were generated to the Saddleback Community Church, asking them politely to, at the least, follow Obama with a speaker who would deconstruct his worldview.

The push for someone to balance Obama's speech failed, and no one was onstage there to present the truth. That's when I penned my column that appeared in December 2006.

Stating clearly that the 2008 election would hinge on five key factors, I argued that the election of Barack Obama as president was unstoppable. Four of the five factors resoundingly rang true: (1) evangelicals listened to emotion rather than fact; (2) African-Americans were energized for the chance at history; (3) Republicans refused to rally to their base with sound conservative principles; and (4) if one of the candidates were John McCain, it would be a shoo-in for Obama (the fifth factor being, moderates were too exhausted to pay attention any further). Political pundits laughed at me for my prediction.

Kellyanne Conway, a talented pollster from New Jersey, cohosted the New York City–based "Ball for Life" with me in 2007. Conway's business depends on her ability to read the electorate, to ask the right questions, and to arrive at reasonably sound expectations for candidates and campaigns. That night, during the reception, we struck up a conversation about the upcoming election. She scoffed at my prediction, stating with great rationale that Hillary Clinton owned the collar (the doughnut-shaped areas around cities) of nearly every county seat in every Democratic district in every state across the nation. Her belief was simple: whoever owned the map won the primary battle.

Her theory still held true, even though Hillary lost and I won the bet.

Obama simply drew himself a new map, caucused in states in which Democrats seldom even campaigned, and not only did he offset Hillary's power within the party infrastructure; he tirelessly raised money so that he could easily outspend her. And then, of course, he kicked in her political teeth in the Iowa primary in the spring of 2008. She never really recovered. But in knocking out the establishment Democratic power title holder and dethroning the former presidential franchise, Obama further seasoned himself to play tough in the general election. Yet as it turned out, he never even needed the practice.

· Republican John McCain led only once in the entire campaign, the week he named Sarah Palin as his VP candidate. Palin was a clear-thinking and clear-speaking evangelical. She was proud of and embraced conservative principles. She drew the excitement of women into the race in ways the GOP had not seen in generations, and she was a compassionate mom who struggled with the issue of fairness for her own special-needs child. Naming Palin as VP was perhaps the only right thing the McCain campaign did.

The day after my column appeared, where I warned that Obama may be unstoppable, talk-radio king Rush Limbaugh read my piece nearly word for word. He echoed the five reasons I had given for Obama's ascendency and then uttered the same sentiment I had at the end of the column: we both hoped I was dreadfully wrong.

I was not.

Realizing that I had accurately predicted the entire process, I genuinely began to dread the future. I actually had thought about a lot more than I had said or written to that point.

The day of Obama's election in November 2008 wasn't even as close as it looked. McCain lost the strongly "red" states of Virginia and North Carolina. The values Obama espoused did not reflect the morality of this part of the country, but they did not know his true character, for he had filled them with the hope that with his ascendency would come the sort of change that would improve their condition and their spirits.

HISTORIC WINS, HUGE EXPECTATIONS

Reflecting on the graciousness Obama showed McCain on election night, and given the fact that I needed to accept the night's outcome as more than merely the act of humankind, but on some level a sign of divine sovereignty, I pledged that from November 2008 until President Obama actually began originating policy ideas that were legitimately unhealthy, I would cease to condemn, critique, or demean him.

I kept my promise. I bit my tongue. I tied my fingers together.

On inauguration day in January 2009, my Facebook community of

7,800 or so weighed in with heavy scorn, resentment, and sarcasm at the "Messiah worship," as many expressed in response to what they felt was slanted media coverage of the event. For the most part I attempted to keep clear of even that, though I did not do so perfectly. Biting my tongue allowed me to do what I suspected the rest of the nation was doing as well: hoping for the signs of hope, the signs of life to return to the American mainstream.

Yet in honesty, I, again, could have predicted exactly what happened.

With such high expectations, no human could live up to them. And it did not take long for America to begin to understand that when they had chanted, "Yes, we can!" in pandemonium in Denver as Obama delivered his acceptance speech in front of the now famous faux Roman columns, it would soon turn into "No, he can't."

Campaign promise after promise being broken in the first few weeks and months of his election soured his political base—including the antiwar, pro-abortion, pro-homosexual, pro-tax, pro-entitlement constituents. Of course, the 43 percent of evangelicals who had believed him were dismayed as he immediately restored funding for overseas abortion and stood on the side of the judicial tyrants in the Prop 8 (a referendum on gay marriage) debate in California.

Yet it was because of his breaking his pledge on taxes—specifically not to raise them on anyone making under $250,000 a year—and later pushing for Congress to pass health care programs that would sizably increase the tax rates on small businesses that the mainstream finally issued their divorce on his policies, while still thinking him a likable chap personally.

And perhaps it is in that enigma that we learn the most about Barack Obama. He is a man who seems to genuinely believe he can help the circumstance of the common man, and he has the oratory skills to sway people who do not know the facts. Yet inside the wrappings, his policies are not just retreads of bygone tax-and-spend eras, but disastrous new policies that will lead to longer seasons of struggle and impoverishment for more individuals than at any time since the Great Depression.

The "audacity of hope" is not found in the current path we're on.

I'm not interested in championing the "Republican message," for the GOP has disappointed nearly as greatly on some of the issues—particularly economic—as the current administration. What I am committed to in the pages ahead is examining through the lens of unrepentant truth where we are, where we were *told* we would be by now, and perhaps how we can get there in spite of the crises we face.

When it comes to our economy, our national defense, and our civil rights, history is not void of answers. We can undo this administration's damage, but first we must learn some important truths. By enacting the rights with which every person was born, by engaging our minds, and by confidently reestablishing the values of freedom, responsibility, and the desire to leave the world better than we found it, we will express loyal opposition to the current state of affairs. But we will do so humbly, thankfully, enthusiastically, and with common sense. Are you ready?

PART ONE

Economics

CHAPTER ONE

Tall Tales About Taxes

Sometimes you just have to speak truth and do it with conviction. If we are to solve the significant challenges facing our economy, our national security, and our civil and moral liberties—and if we are to take stewardship of our world seriously—we're going to have to use bare-knuckled truth when we oppose popular political expression and the dishonesty found within it. To be clear, it is important when speaking of policy and its consequences to be accurate and honest.

So in my opinion, when it comes to economic policy, President Barack Obama has failed miserably to do so.

Beginning back when he was presidential-candidate Obama, he began laying down the long litany of falsehoods about the taxes being paid by American citizens, and the ridiculous, unaccountable spending that has gone hand in hand with them is one of the great travesties of modern times.

In the midst of an economy that was tightening, when then candidate Obama declared repeatedly that the tax cuts passed by a bipartisan Congress and signed into law during the Bush administration were nothing more than "tax cuts for the wealthy," it was dishonest. When he asserted

and reasserted that the country had been damaged by the prior administration and that the economic slowdown was evidence of it, that, too, was
dishonest. When he assured Americans that letting the tax relief—pushed
for so strongly by President Bush—expire would be a healthy thing for the
American economy, again it was dishonest.

But this was dishonesty that helped him win the election.

Leftist progressives like Barack Obama believe that the attainment of
power is such a crucial principle that using any means necessary to gain
it is permissible. We will discuss this in much greater detail throughout
this book, but for now understand the simple fact that President Obama
knew as a candidate that the policies he claimed would work had been
proven historically as failures. Yet because of his dishonest representa-
tion of those policies, he was able to claim the mantle of power and earn
forgiveness in the eyes of the Left. But that is the unfortunate side effect
of dishonesty. Once you begin, it's difficult to stop, and eventually it
begins to unwrap around you.

Unfortunately for many, it did not take long to see the lies begin to
unfurl, even among ardent Obama campaign supporters.

OVERPROMISE, UNDER-DELIVER

Have you ever ordered an item after watching an infomercial about it?
On screen the charming spokesman explains over and over how this one
item will solve all of your problems and then some. "But wait; there's
more!" he tells you when you reach for the remote. Even though in your
heart of hearts you know it's simply too good to be true, and that nothing could deliver on those promises, you allow yourself to be hopeful, to
be taken in, and you pull out your Visa card and call that 800 number.

This was the exact tactic taken by the Obama administration in
2008. Consistently staying on a message with a "too good to be true"
ring to it, day after day. And it worked! Millions of Americans went to
the voting booth and pulled the lever for Barack Obama, sometimes even

admitting after doing so that they had no idea how he would live up to his promises.

For them the ushering in of the era that was sold as "Hope and Change" was more important than having a firm grasp of whether or not it would happen.

Throughout the campaign, one of the significant criticisms in my own mind as to Barack Obama's weakness as a leader was the fact that he had little-to-no executive experience outside of political campaigns. Time and again when challenged on this issue of executive experience, something that was equally lacking in both of the general election candidates of 2008, Obama's retort would be a reference to the size, scope, and success of his campaign operation.

In his column for the *Washington Examiner* dated June 8, 2010, Byron York documented two such references:

> In mid-February 2008, fresh from winning a bunch of Super Tuesday primaries, Barack Obama granted an interview to "60 Minutes" correspondent Steve Croft. "When you sit down and you look at [your] resume," Croft said to Obama, "there's no executive experience, and in fact, correct [me] if I'm wrong, the only thing that you've actually run was the Harvard Law Review."
>
> "Well, I've run my Senate office, and I've run this campaign," Obama said.
>
> Seven months later, after receiving the Democratic presidential nomination, Obama talked with CNN's Anderson Cooper. At the time, the news was dominated by Hurricane Gustav, which was headed toward New Orleans and threatening to become a Katrina-like disaster. "Some of your Republican critics have said you don't have the experience to handle a situation like this," Cooper said to Obama. "They in fact have said that Governor Palin has more executive experience . . ."
>
> "Governor Palin's town of Wasilla has, I think, 50 employees," Obama answered. "We have got 2,500 in this campaign. I think their budget is maybe $12 million a year. You know, we have a budget of

about three times that just for the month. So, I think that our ability to manage large systems and to execute, I think, has been made clear over the last couple of years."[1]

So we are to understand that Obama was willing to be judged by his track record at the helm of his electoral campaign operation as a measure of how he would ultimately run the nation?

Little did any of us know how prophetic that assumption truly was.

I WANT MY MONEY TODAY!

Very few newspapers ran the story when the news broke in the first week of November 2008.

People who had logged thousands of hours going door-to-door urging people to vote for Obama, driving people to the polls on election day, blanketing the byways with last-minute yard signs—and in Philadelphia, standing shoulder to shoulder to prevent Republicans from voting—suddenly got a taste of the hope and change Obama had long since promised: he didn't have money to pay them for their work.

Not surprisingly some of the campaign workers took umbrage to explanations the campaign gave them and began marching on the local offices. Several hundred disenfranchised Obama campaign staffers took to protesting right outside the doors of the local Obama election office in Indianapolis. Some shrieked and screamed at the media, "I want my money today! It's my money. I want it right now!"

Some of the 375 unpaid staffers were offered a $30 prepaid Visa. In some cases those staffers had worked weeks without paychecks, setting up events, recruiting attendance to rallies, and ultimately attempting to gain Obama the public's trust. In those speeches, at those rallies, and while shaking their hands, he promised economic recovery through specific ideas and plans that, in the opinion of history, he already knew had failed in the past. How ironic that the very first people to feel the sting of that dishonest message were the pawns in the game that had specifically been used to carry the water.

How bad did they feel when they realized the day after the election was over, when they were told, "Hey instead of your paycheck, here's a $30 prepaid Visa, and we really appreciate all your help"?

The falsehood of the "overpromise" was probably the most stinging to a poor woman who gained fame on YouTube.[2] Her name is Peggy Joseph. And after attending an Obama/Biden rally in Kansas City, she made her now infamous comment to the watching world, saying that if she would just help Obama, he would see to it that she had gas in her tank and that her mortgage was paid.

At the time of this writing, President Obama has delivered on neither of those promises. And therein lies a larger issue. If he knows that the plans with which he has aligned himself to "fix" the "worst recession since the Great Depression" will not work, why risk the inevitable damage to his reputation in the end?

President Obama made the rookiest of all rookie errors while rushing his ascendency to 1600 Pennsylvania Avenue: he has overpromised and underdelivered. And now that the economy has stagnated to this level, one must wonder what else he has planned.

Unfortunately, there's plenty more he could do . . .

A TAX INCREASE BY ANY OTHER NAME

It was the campaign pledge heard 'round the globe.

"How many people in here make less than a quarter million dollars a year?" Senator Barack Obama would call out at the same point in every campaign speech. "Uh-huh . . . that's what I thought. Well if you make less than a quarter million dollars a year, in a Barack Obama administration, you will not see your taxes increase by a single dime. And 95 percent of Americans will see their taxes go down."[3]

Because so many who heard him on the campaign trail never took a look at the fine print of his policy goals, they did not realize that he was planning to break that same promise before even concluding the speech through which they were sitting at that very moment.

Oddly enough it is a campaign pledge he has claimed to keep even after election. He referred to it in his State of the Union address in 2010:

> That's why we extended or increased unemployment benefits for more than 18 million Americans; made health insurance 65 percent cheaper for families who get their coverage through COBRA; and passed 25 different tax cuts.
>
> Now, let me repeat: We cut taxes. We cut taxes for 95 percent of working families. (Applause.) We cut taxes for small businesses. We cut taxes for first-time homebuyers. We cut taxes for parents trying to care for their children. We cut taxes for 8 million Americans paying for college. (Applause.)[4]

The only problem with his reference is that it was 100 percent untrue. It was untrue in January 2009, and remains so even now.

In order to justify his numbers, Obama's accounting took funny math and applied it to a round of checks that were sent to the American people as a form of welfare. Yet in reality those rounds of payment could not under any honest accounting be considered tax cuts. The tax rates themselves were not reduced, and from the moment President Obama made the "anyone making less than $250,000" pledge, Americans could expect to be told in that same speech that tax increases were on the way.

So let's press Pause for a moment and demonstrate how these promises were false.

From the same campaign podiums that President Obama proffered his own "no new taxes" pledge on those making less than a quarter of a million dollars per year, he also attempted to indemnify honest tax relief passed in the previous administration.

"The Bush Tax Cuts for the Wealthy" was how he referred to the series of genuine tax reductions that had been passed by Democrats and

Republicans working together in the previous administration and signed into law by then president George W. Bush. With bipartisan support President Bush had pushed for a reduction in the marriage penalty, the estate tax, federal income taxes, and a host of taxes related to the average American's retirement savings and investment plans.

Did the Bush tax reductions benefit the wealthy? Of course they did. But they also benefited every American household that paid federal taxes.

What President Obama never revealed as a candidate, and in my opinion, will not bother to volunteer now that he holds office, is that for the total amount of tax revenues paid to the federal treasury, those evil wealthy people pay roughly 50 percent of the total federal tax receipts. Additionally at the time of the election, the bottom 45 percent of earners in the American economy had a 0 percent federal tax burden to pay.

These parameters become highly important given the dynamics of the psychology of his pledge on the campaign trail. For if 45 percent of workers are not paying federal taxes, how is it possible that 95 percent of American working families would receive tax reductions?

What President Obama distributed in the form of the federal checks sent within the first few months of his presidency was not a reduction of tax rates that were in place; it was payback for votes that had been cast to get him elected. And the majority of it went to people who did not presently pay federal taxes.

Additionally, when Candidate Obama would excoriate the Bush-Tax-Cuts-for-the-Wealthy, he normally followed it up with a pledge to allow them to expire in 2010. Somehow he believed that if they simply expired, it would remove his responsibility from the equation of ushering in one of the largest tax increases in history (which it will be).

But if you will notice his promise made in the statement at the first of this section, he didn't promise that he wouldn't raise taxes. He promised that people's taxes wouldn't increase by a dime on his administration's watch. In the most specific and literal sense of the words he spoke, it would be his duty to *oppose* the expiration of the Bush tax cuts, not to allow them to expire.

Yet by clearly stating his intention to watch them expire, Senator Obama, candidate for the presidency, was fully announcing tax increases, not only on the top 2 percent of earners, but on every tax-paying working family in America. The very same working families that he pledged would not see their taxes increase by a "single dime."

New York Post: 57 Percent Tax Rates for Small Businesses

There is no greater way to injure the working family in America than to smash the kneecaps of American small business. Small businesses in America account for roughly two out of every three new jobs created in the modern economy. At times in our history, that number has increased to as many as three of every four.

Many small-business owners make less than $250,000 in revenue per year, and a large number of businesses clear less than that in total profits. Needless to say, many—if not the majority of—small businesses in America would potentially have felt some measure of security in Candidate Obama's promise to not allow a "single dime's" increase in the taxes they pay.

So imagine the shock to those same small-business owners when they opened up the *New York Post* on July 22, 2009, where Charlie Hurt began his report:

> Congressional plans to fund a massive health-care overhaul could have a job-killing effect on New York, creating a tax rate of nearly 60 percent for the state's top earners and possibly pressuring small-business owners to shed workers.
>
> New York's top income bracket could reach as high as 57 percent— rates not seen in three decades—to pay for the massive health coverage proposed by House Democrats this week.
>
> The top rate in New York City, home to many of the state's wealthiest people, would be 58.68 percent, the Washington-based Tax Foundation said in a report yesterday.
>
> That means New York's top earners, small-business owners and most dynamic entrepreneurs will be facing new fees and penalties.

The non-partisan think-tank calculated the average local tax rate in New York State at 1.7 percent, and combined it with the 8.97 percent that high-bracket state taxpayers will shell out in 2011, when the health care plan is set to take effect. Tack on the 39.6 percent federal tax rate, 2.9 percent for Medicare and 5.4 percent for the health care "surtax," and the figure is 56.92 percent for the Empire State.

In New York City, the top tax rate is 3.65 percent, making the Big Apple's top combined rate even higher.

The $544 billion tax hike would violate one of President Obama's ironclad campaign promises: No family will pay higher tax rates than they would have paid in the 1990s.

Under the bill, three new tax brackets would be created for high earners, with a top rate of 45 percent for families making more than $1 million. That would be the highest income-tax rate since 1986, when the top rate was 50 percent.

The legislation is especially onerous for business owners, in part because it penalizes employers some 8 percent of wages if they don't offer health care.

But the cost of the buy-in to the program may be so prohibitive that it will dissuade owners from growing their businesses—a scary prospect in the midst of a recession.[5]

A scary prospect indeed! When the health care bill became law, the possible 60 percent tax rate for the very sector of the society that needed to be growing its employee base, had a chokehold placed on it.

But that was 2009. When the tax rates revert to Clintonian levels in 2011 (which will happen when the "Bush Tax Cuts" expire) and beyond, it will have a chilling effect on job creation by businesses small and large. That will make a bad situation even worse for those without work.

Around this same time period in 2009, members of the White House press corps began putting two and two together. They were beginning to very slowly realize that perhaps what had been promised prior to November 2008 wasn't quite measuring up in post-January 2009.

OBAMA: READ MY LIPS

As someone who had followed Barack Obama's political career closely, I expected him to slow his pace to the left once he was elected president, as most liberal candidates have done in the past. That is to say he would move more deliberately and cautiously on a liberal agenda once elected.

But President Obama surprised me with his willingness to believe his administration's own press. For months on end, we as a nation were told that this president had more to accomplish because of the enormity of the challenges he would find once in office, and that because of these challenges, the American people would need to be patient as they waited for solutions to problems and improvement in the life of the nation.

When it comes to a president's ability to influence the nation's economy, Democrat John F. Kennedy and Republican Ronald W. Reagan had something in common. They both believed that if government spending could be restrained, and the largest marginal tax rates were reduced, then economic recovery and growth would become a bipartisan by-product of the habits of a free market.

Any observer of the increasingly tight markets, continued lack of jobs, and general malaise of the presently disillusioned workforce could tell you that President Obama's response has been the exact opposite of JFK and Reagan's. Obama has given guidance and direction to the largest "bloatation" of government spending in the history of our nation. In fact, the amount of federal money spent during his first six months in office was more than what we'd spent in the entirety of America's history in terms of gross numbers of dollars allocated.

The insufferable truth being told, his administration, more than any before, sought to weaken, limit, and control the free market. By way of illustration, he appointed more czars (32) in oversight positions than the number of weeks he'd been in office (22). Had he maintained that pace, by the end of his term, he'd have appointed roughly a grand total of 256 czars.

One of Obama's many goals is to enact "cap and trade," a complex system of taxes and carbon credits that would result in higher taxes for companies using traditional energy sources. (More on this to come.) It amounted to the largest and most punitive tax increase ever formulated, and it would affect everyone, especially the poorest and neediest citizens. The entire basis for the existence of cap and trade is that carbon—what we exhale when we breathe—damages our environment. That theory is inconclusive and far from agreed upon among the science community, much less the American people.

President Obama falsely argued that cap and trade would not be felt by the taxpayer earning under $250,000 a year. He claimed that corporations would be the ones to foot the bill for the penalties for imaginary carbon credits. Yet he failed to notify the American taxpayer that companies never pay taxes.

Yes, you read that right.

Companies do one of two things when they are assigned a new tax: they pass the cost on to the customer, or they go out of business. Since most corporations are not looking to go out of business and thus lay off their entire workforce, they are forced to pass that tax on to the customer, every time, without exception.

None of what I've just described has been anything but an attempt by President Obama to make good on promises he made during his run for office. Even his promise of universal health care was an attempt on some level to keep such a promise.

But then there's the little issue of how to pay for it. And on this point President Obama signaled the reality that he would break the biggest campaign promise he had made.

The White House press corps specifically drew blood in the water on the health care expense at the end of June 2009, forcing the administration to admit that if it were in fact necessary, President Obama would raise taxes on those making less than $250,000 a year to make it happen. Thus the biggest promise repeated over and over in every corner of the nation became meaningless: as ephemeral as a batch of cotton candy, it disappeared the moment it left the tongue.

It is the historical equivalent of what happened when President

George H. W. Bush ran for his second term against Governor Clinton. He had promised, "Read my lips: no new taxes" in his run against Michael Dukakis only to go down in historic defeat in his bid for re-election for later going back on the promise.

For President Obama "not one single dime" is the new standard, and given the approval ratings slip that began to follow, it became evident that those who made under $250,000 were beginning to understand that they'd been had.

ALL POLITICS ARE POCKETBOOK

For President Obama, history will judge his effectiveness in office by how the ideas and policies for which he campaigned and worked to pass impacted the American worker. In this respect, his approach to selling one tax message to the American voter—but knowing from the inception it would not deliver the goods—was a strategy of failure. Furthermore, I believe it fundamentally established failure in nearly every other area of governance for which he'd set goals.

No policy in America is as broadly punitive to the working family of America as gross increases in taxation. No policy hurts the population in general more than punitive taxes on the American small business community. And nothing in terms of economic policy prevents the nation from improving its economic quality of life for the average American more than wrestling away from us the control over the dollars we earn.

With President Obama's bait-and-switch tax policy, he set himself up for failure in other arenas. The pain on the American voter's life was exacerbated as reality began to bash into the fantasy of change that would be full of hope and bring them to a better economic reality.

And so the tall tales were told.

CHAPTER TWO

Bailouts to Stimulus, Making the Pie Smaller

It was a statement said with such force and vigor that it was designed to send chills down the spines of all who heard it. Even for those of us who knew the truth behind the words, it had a ring of horror. It gave the new administration a perceived mandate. It allowed an Obama senior adviser to render the instruction to "never allow a good crisis to go to waste." And it resulted in the first major piece of legislation newly sworn-in President Barack Obama was to sign into law.

The statement paraphrased simply: "We were bleeding jobs at a rate of 750,000 per month the January I was sworn in."

In this one statement, which was only true for a single-month period (and technically speaking, a portion of that month was on Obama's watch), the president chided, cajoled, and pleaded with Congress to pass $1.3 trillion worth of stimulus relief. It was also the single largest domestic spending program to date in non-budgetary, non-defense-related allocation of tax dollars in U.S. history.

15

There were many reasons to oppose the stimulus bill, cleverly renamed "the American Recovery Act" before it was passed. But the months since its passing tell a more exacting story, a tale of absolute graft, waste, corruption, fraud, and incompetence in the use of public money. Not to mention that we had to borrow much of it from other countries, like China, to whom we and our children's children's children are now indebted. It will literally take generations of American taxes to pay back the stimulus money. A good portion of it also came from overprinting our own currency, which historically always leads to inflation at some point.

The stimulus bill is now a documented failure. But that is not what President Obama claimed some two years after its passage, during the 2010 State of the Union address:

> Because of the steps we took, there are about two million Americans working right now who would otherwise be unemployed. (Applause.) Two hundred thousand work in construction and clean energy; 300,000 are teachers and other education workers. Tens of thousands are cops, firefighters, correctional officers, first responders. (Applause.) And we're on track to add another one and a half million jobs to this total by the end of the year.
>
> The plan that has made all of this possible, from the tax cuts to the jobs, is the Recovery Act. (Applause.) That's right—the Recovery Act, also known as the stimulus bill. (Applause.) Economists on the left and the right say this bill has helped save jobs and avert disaster. But you don't have to take their word for it. Talk to the small business in Phoenix that will triple its workforce because of the Recovery Act. Talk to the window manufacturer in Philadelphia who said he used to be skeptical about the Recovery Act, until he had to add two more work shifts just because of the business it created. Talk to the single teacher raising two kids who was told by her principal in the last week of school that because of the Recovery Act, she wouldn't be laid off after all.[1]

In order to demonstrate a bit more, let's examine a little closer.

CONDOMS AND WATER PARKS
V. $17,000 PER FAMILY

It'd been a tough three weeks on the job for Mr. President.

In breaking news on the afternoon of Friday, February 6, 2009, CBS News reported a startling conclusion: Mr. Obama's stimulus—97 percent of which would be disbursed through additional federal spending—was the exact opposite of how most Americans felt the economic crisis should be handled. In their findings CBS reported that 59 percent of the nation believed the relief package should focus primarily, if not entirely, on real, honest-to-goodness tax-rate reductions.

We all do remember that he campaigned on this, right? That under the Obama economic plan, he would begin economic recovery by *cutting the taxes* of 95 percent of Americans?

Yet despite economic advisers telling him otherwise, despite the Reagan biographies he claimed to be reading following his election, despite the fact that the brightest economic minds in the nation advocated differently, and by then despite the fact that the American people had contrarily advised (the CBS News poll found that only 22 percent thought more government spending would solve the economic crisis),[2] Mr. Obama, Nancy Pelosi, and Harry Reid believed it was more important to spend nearly $1.3 trillion in stimulus allocation than to do the only thing that would allow the economy to recover.

This was likely their prescribed goal all along.

An economy that heals by allowing the workers and producers in this nation to keep what they have earned, invest it in new growth, add jobs to the private sector, and expand production in America, was the greatest thing liberal party leaders had to fear.

For the record, I opposed all of our bailout and stimulus efforts from the very first ones in mid-2008. I'd repeatedly written and advocated on Fox News, radio, and elsewhere that bailouts (artificial props under poorly performing companies) never succeed, and the price of not allowing failure merely would extend the long term-losses.

But give Obama and company benefit of the doubt for a moment, just for the sake of argument. Let's argue that the government taking $1.3 trillion in taxes from us will turn things around. How, then, should it be spent?

What had emerged from the House and Senate proceedings was a slab of pork spending so large in scope that the average taxpayer gasped with offense when the final list was revealed. (Millions for condoms, hundreds of millions for STD awareness, even rumored water parks for Florida.) The ludicrously large $1.3 trillion sounds like pretend money in some board game. It's impossible to get your mind around a sum like that.

Most people do not realize that $1.3 trillion was more money than if one had spent $1 million a day since the birth of Christ right up to February 8, 2009. If you break it down across the raw population of America (not voters, not taxpayers, not even just adults, but *everyone*), it would average out to roughly $4,290 per person. A married couple would garner a touch more than $8,500. A family of four comes in at just over $17,000. And that's just the principal. Not the interest.

At a dinner party in Chicago the previous week, I asked the four couples gathered around the table what they would do with that amount of money coming back to them from the government. They all mentioned home projects, fix-me-up stuff, and goods they needed, and some mentioned paying off debt. They also listed new, big-ticket home electronic items, and the ladies around the table all daydreamed momentarily of a spa day. Long story short, every item they talked about would have employed someone like a contractor, plumber, or electrician. They would have added to the welfare of commerce—big-ticket items, new transportation, spa services, etc. And some would have even helped solidify the crumbling credit market by paying off credit card balances and putting cash back into the system.

If this was the case with merely five couples of very modest means, imagine the heat that would warm the economic engine from an entire nation responding this way. America would've never seen this kind of stimulus put in place before. The largest tax cuts that President Bush instituted were roughly $1,500 per family. The amount of fluidity this plan would free up would be more than ten times that amount. Put another way, do you know any struggling families of four that could use $17,000? Think it would mean anything to them?

President Obama's bad missteps the week that Congress passed the stimulus bill were confounded not just by horrendously partisan policy-making, but also by the arrogance with which he penned an op-ed in the *Washington Post* and gave a retreat address to House Democrats. (Some of these same Democrats are pleading with him not to pursue the federal spending but to replace it with tax relief, or credits, or whatever Obama's term for it would be this go-around.)

President Obama is not a king; he is a servant, as every leader should be. He's the employee that we citizens hired to administrate the nation for the next four years. His power exists only at the discretion of "We the People." And when he spurns the majority of the nation on the single greatest domestic issue facing us, he'd be wise to stop wagging his finger at us, and begin some of that "listening to us" that he promised us in nearly twenty-four months of campaigning.

It will also be good to keep in mind the comparative value of $17,000 per family versus condoms, STDs, and water parks, since the struggle for economic recovery has still not taken a turn for the better as of the writing of this text.

SWIFT FEEDBACK FOR A CLUELESS CEO

What began to emerge following the passage of stimulus was an interesting phenomenon. A new trend in Obama's rating betrayed a chink in his political armor, and the early cracks indicated that Obama's likable personality might not be the best match for the job of CEO of the free world. The passage of the act had told the American people something: while they thought he was a decent human being, he didn't particularly wish to listen to them.

Exit polling in the court of public opinion proved that when he had said, "Hope and Change" on the campaign trail, the voters assumed they meant the same thing, when in fact what he meant was, in some cases, wildly, polarizingly opposite.

Poll numbers had plagued Obama's predecessor. Contrasting himself favorably to the Bush team repeatedly seemed to work. Little did he realize the overreach this ploy would cost him, for within fifty days of occupying the White House, Obama's job approval numbers had registered lower than George W. Bush's, though you would've been hard-pressed to see it reported very many places.

There was much more to the fact that President Obama polled lower than President Bush did at fifty days into his presidency than merely what bipartisan pollsters Schoen and Rasmussen were able to point out the week of March 15, 2009.[3] The two pollsters—one an Independent and one a Democrat—had conducted a series of polls on a host of issues, including national security, foreign affairs, domestic employment, economic vitality, and optimism for the future.

In nearly every category of performance, the polls showed that people believed President Obama had adeptly demonstrated that he was in over his head, and sinking fast. "We the people" were growing uneasy with his inability to make sound decisions. The president had wiped out nearly all of the Republican support he had enjoyed not long before, and Independents were not far behind.

When you considered the sector of the Democratic base that believed raising taxes on everyday working people is bad, you even began to see a schism in his base not previously thought to be possible. At the end of the day, something had to change. Either President Obama would choose to formulate new policies, or "We the People" would use a shepherd's staff first in 2010, then in 2012.

In my syndicated column I had been tracking the number of campaign promises that he had broken to date. Yet many of these didn't even rise to half the level of importance on the issues that we were growing increasingly concerned about.

IT'S THE JOBS, STUPID!

To be perfectly frank, nothing much mattered at that snapshot in time besides the economy, job loss, and the bleak prospects of anything changing in the near future. The American people were watching their newly elected "historic" president go on national television nearly three times a week, yet his answers to the most pressing questions on their minds brought them little comfort. For the first time his job approval numbers headed toward territory that President Bush did not see until deep into his second term.

Prior to the completion of the campaign, President Obama promised that jobs would begin to be created. He reiterated this after the election. As it impacted the economy specifically, the authors of the stimulus had promised steady but slow job growth. The term "shovel-ready projects" was attached to nearly every discussion, and in fact was one of the major points argued in favor of a swift passage.

Yet in reality something else altogether was happening. The unemployment numbers had skyrocketed, escalating especially hard following the signing of his stimulus plan. The plan, according to leading economists, only dedicated roughly 3 percent of the total amount toward actual job creation.

On this point Warren Buffet, one of President Obama's strong campaign supporters, expressed grave reservations. The American billionaire went public to state his disagreement, one of the first to do so in those first fifty days. Buffet also understood something else that he was witnessing from the Obama administration. Something especially evident on economic policy following the passage of stimulus. Something troubling: when it came to criticism, Obama was stiff-necked.

Early on, President Obama could easily dismiss such commentary if it came only from conservative punditry circles, but even with Buffet's departure, the administration felt that trudging forward to implement their campaign agenda would eventually win the hearts of those who did not support them.

Because stimulus was supposed to have "fixed" the jobs picture, Obama made the calculated decision to move forward with two other agenda items: health care and cap-and-trade legislation were drawn up and introduced in the House. Pressing full steam ahead on both items, Obama found himself in the unenviable position of not having yet fully secured victory on the first front, while opening two more major campaigns on the battlefield of ideas and policy. From a sheer political standpoint, it was always risky to be so ambitious. But to take this amount of risk within a fifty-day window of time verged on foolish—in political terms.

I wrote from the very beginning of his term that it would be important for him to attack his agenda in such a way that the American people would be in support of it, if he wished to be successful. It would have been a difficult sell even in a prosperous year. But candidate Obama had just taken the previous two years to pound into our hearts and minds that we were captive to an economy that was supposedly the worst since the Great Depression of the 1930s and '40s.

After the stimulus Barack Obama pivoted away from jobs, the economy, and financial relief altogether. As though he were living in a bubble, his conversation turned to health care, while the American people watched as weekly the 8 percent unemployment that he promised turned into 8.2, then 8.7, then 9.0, 9.5, 9.7, and eventually 10 percent.

"Underemployment" is the term for the number of people who have work but are out of money before their basic needs are met. Under President Bush the number ranged from one in seventeen to one in twenty families that suffered through this type of week-to-week existence. But under Barack Obama, that number ballooned fast, all the way to nearly one in five families.

It seemed that in President Obama's mind, passing the stimulus equated to solving the long-term economic problems. Further, once those problems were solved, it would free him up to focus on the other items.

It was a pivot he should not have made, and he will pay a price for it.

Obama should have made job creation his singular focus. He claimed to do just that, and it would've been wonderful if it had been true. But the fact is he did not. Jobs would have created health care for every person who wound up with job-sponsored health benefits. Jobs would have grown the federal treasury for incoming receipts because it would have been growing the number of employed taxpayers. Fixing the jobs numbers through genuine reform would have helped businesses stay competitive by hiring effective work staffs. Yet because President Obama believed that spending $1.3 trillion of tax money we didn't have would fix that issue, instead, things got worse.

If video killed the radio star, in the words of the old pop tune,[4] then Obama killed the jobs star, and was never able to relight it.

POLLING: THE REST OF THE STORY

Pollsters Rasmussen and Schoen were able to turn up a good number of other things; here were some of the additional disconnects:

- In my opinion, one of the great lies that President Obama continued to try to perpetuate is that "going green" would jump-start economic growth. At the same time, he restated in his address to Congress what he had said on the campaign trail: that no family earning less than $250,000 would see an increase in taxes. Yet every family in America was going to pay additional tax under his cap-and-trade program. By essentially punishing evil big business for carbon footprints, the feds claim they would tax said "evil" businesses to show them who's boss. Oddly enough, those "evil" businesses will never feel the sting because they will pass the cost of the imposed taxes on to the consumer in the form of higher prices for simple things like electricity, natural gas, and whatever other forms of energy they may use.

- On foreign relations he spoke loud and long about improving the reputation of the United States globally. He promptly began his administration by giving the very first sit-down interviews to networks run by our enemies (Al Jazeera television). He then thrice insulted Great Britain, our closest ally. He was left with major distance between his wishes and those of Israel, our closest ally in the Middle East. And topping it off, his administration dealt with Brazil, our closest South American ally, with the same kind of "White House gift shop" hospitality with which he had just kicked Great Britain in the knee.
- On national security, Venezuela's Hugo Chavez taunted him, North Korea threatened him, Iran burned him in effigy, and Russia, Cuba, and Venezuela are plotting ways to put Russian long-range bombers in our hemisphere and directly off our coast.
- On terrorism, Iran, Al-Qaeda, and bin Laden openly mock him. Maybe his giving Hamas—a terror group on the international terror watch list—$90 million wasn't quite the bold stroke of genius his cabinet told him it would be.

No doubt, however, President Obama's most pressing problem with the public was still the fact that even after the first fifty days of his term, 83 percent of Americans said they are worried that the steps he had taken to "fix" the economy would have the opposite effect and make things worse. About the same percentage said they were worried about the monstrous rise in the national debt. Slightly fewer believed inflation would come quickly. And 69 percent did not have any confidence in the role of government-mandated solutions to the economy. There was also now no sense that the stimulus would have any positive effect anytime soon. Only 60 percent held out hope that it would have any impact realized four years from then. Most important, by a margin of 12 percent, the American people believed the stimulus would only help and unfairly benefit those who had already been irresponsible.

Americans had heard the word "crisis" roll off the lips of the administration like syrup in those days. But now, President Obama had one of his own. His policies were failing in every direction.

MINI-STIMULUS: CASH FOR CLUNKERS

If there were a single event in the early part of 2009 that seemed to show the desperately out-of-touch nature of the Obama administration, it was a disastrously named campaign called "Cash for clunkers."

Just imagine . . .

Imagine the government making an estimable promise of enormous proportion. Imagine the government pledging a promise so big that it would, in fact, as they would argue, actually save an entire sector of the economy.

We're talking about a program that uses our tax dollars to purchase cars that cannot be resold and that no one will drive, but will instead be taken directly to the nearest junkyard and crushed. And imagine if, after promising this program would last for a long period of time, it ran out of actual cash in about one-sixteenth of the time they pledged it would work. While they promised there would be enough of our tax dollars—for which we slaved at our jobs, to feed our families—to cause the program to last until November, maybe even through the end of the year, they blew it in not even one full week's time.

That's how your government spent $1 billion in roughly six days in 2009.

They called it an "economic stimulus" designed to boost the purchasing of American-made, more fuel-efficient vehicles. Of course they had boosted the sales of these vehicles artificially. Instead of letting the manufacturers do what every other company has to do when it makes vehicles, products, or widgets that nobody wants—fold—they instead felt compelled to encourage you to "buy" a vehicle that nobody was buying, and to then use our tax dollars to buy your clunker.

So you and I, the taxpayers, bought 240,000 clunkers in six days, of

25

which roughly 80 percent had already been eliminated from circulation at our local junk heaps before that week's end. And did people get a good deal on the cars they bought? No! Because instead of buying something that they had saved for, the vast majority of these purchasers were actually buying extended indebtedness agreements to the dealer. Meaning that the new cars being purchased were for the most part being financed, on the buyer's credit, and the government's promise to the local dealer. The dealers must have felt as though they were having to sell their souls to President Obama just to stay in business.

To top it off, New York senator Chuck Schumer and several Democrats in the House, including Barney Frank and Maxine Waters, had commanded the gerbil-operated printing press in the White House basement to print up $2 billion more so that you and I could hopefully buy somewhere in the vicinity of 750,000 clunkers. Then they doled out selectively—randomly, if you asked the dealerships—$2 billion that had belonged to "We the People," in exchange for three quarters of a million dollars' worth of junked cars. The Obama administration promised that this little effort would save the auto industry. They'd promised it would save the environment. But what about saving the taxpayer's dinner for his or her children?

Strikingly at that point in time in 2009, I became aware of a little fact that I repeated often on Fox News in those days: Did you know that if you flushed $1 million a day down the toilet from the day Jesus Christ was born until the time the "Cash for Clunkers" program kicked in, you would've barely spent more than $7 billion?

The Obama administration had long since passed that number in spending on stimulus alone, but now to add another $2 billion on top of that would only have the expected effect on the markets. Everything froze, and stayed frozen for a number of weeks.

Mr. Obama was in many places being seen doing many things during this six-day episode, all the while making strong assurances that his administration would make *certain* that his *promises* to the American health care system would only *improve* in the days to come. Many of us walked away wondering, *How do we know you will do any better by us than making us pay for junk?*

Our own eyes had just watched it happen.

TRUTH BE TOLD

The general methodology of attempting to spur the economy into vibrant stability by massive spending measures more or less died a long, excruciating death between the bailouts and stimulus early on, and then in more pronounced ways on items like "cash for clunkers." But the reasons it does not work are not new.

President Obama, from the day he took office, seemed to believe in a Utopia that he still sees in his mind today. It is a happy picture, where hunger, homelessness, heartache, and heartburn do not exist. But that is nothing like the place where you and I live. We know, for example, that we are required to pay our bills and to pay them on time each month. We know that if we do not, we will accumulate more debt than we will be able to pay for.

Now, does that mean that our buying things doesn't help the overall economy? Of course not. But buying them when we do not have means to do so creates indentured servitude. The debts we see modeled in the massive spending programs by the federal government are by example saying to us, "You don't have to pay your bills. Keep spending, and it will all turn out well in the end."

But if you don't subscribe to the theory of massive consumption, then you know that the truth is taking you to a more responsible place. A place of honor, of distinction, of economic safety.

What Obama's team does not do well is disguise their contempt for all other ideas outside of their own massive spending plans. And economics is not the only place their lips curl.

27

CHAPTER
THREE

Punishing the Wealthy, Despising the Poor

It was pretty obvious from his earliest days on the campaign trail through his inauguration that President Barack Obama was not one to reject the instinct to engage in class warfare. He was especially disinclined to do so if it furthered his credibility with specific demographics. And while it was often dressed up in the language of 2008, his verbal attempts to divide Americans poor against rich were almost completely unoriginal.

Sad to say, he was quite successful in his rhetoric and tone. And due to the fact that we as Americans have grown sadly illiterate in our study of history, few had the discernment to see through the president's ploy. But we should have.

Knowing that if he could pit the nation's inner cities against the geographically less dense towns, suburbs, and villages of America, he planned on creating an angst in the heart of the middle class to see themselves as poor, the poor to see themselves as destitute, and the "wealthy" to avoid anyone knowing they're well-off.

In short his desire was to shame the successful. To cause people to look at what the fruit of others' labor produced and to believe that it was ill-gotten even if it had been earned honestly. The reason he wished them to do so was simple: he wanted to win.

But getting people to despise success would assist him in the implementation of his agenda once in office—or so he believed—so allowing the cloud of suspicion to hang over anyone making more than $24,000 (the poverty line for a family of four) a year was something he was comfortable with. Unfortunately, it also exploited those on whom he most depended to create the public outcry and demand for dependency upon his agenda. And instead of setting people free—the genuine benefit of free-market capitalism—he was content to economically enslave people.

From the very beginning, Obama and others, such as White House press secretary Robert Gibbs and chief of staff David Axelrod, drove the message of Obama as "the savior" to those who lived in poverty. The sinister reality was that he would get elected by standing on the shoulders of the poor, and then do all he could to keep them there.

EXPLOITING THE PLIGHT OF THE POOR

We heard a lot about those who were unable to "make it in America" during the 2008 campaign. Despite the clear record of opportunity that America has delivered, and despite the fact that people across every race and nationality have found success here, we were reminded again and again from then candidate Obama that poor people still exist. We were told a lot of things about them as well.

We were told that they were inept in their efforts to help themselves. They were too dumb to make clear choices. We were told constantly that the only way to help them is to grow government. Democrats, and the progressive Left in particular, exploit the poor; they write speeches about them and manipulate their "unrepresented voices" in debates.

But one thing became increasingly clear from the Obama administration and the popular Left in America: in my opinion, at least, they haven't had in the past and they do not now have any interest in genuinely helping the poor.

It is easy to see this looking at the president's policies from a macro-worldview position. Neither the bailout, the stimulus, the omnibus (all-inclusive spending plan), nor the proposed budget (which ended up never being passed) did anything to assist a poor person in finding independence. Securing a dependency upon government handouts, yes. Securing a voting bloc to keep putting politicians in power, yes. But finding genuine liberty, economically speaking, not a chance.

All of these policies aimed to create an enslavement to entitlements that dehumanize the individual, create embarrassment for his or her family, and ultimately rob that person of one of the most cherished gifts God grants us: the satisfaction of personal achievement.

But moving beyond Obama's budget policies, the administration attempted to team up to do what could only injure the poor families of America with the program of "cap and trade." Labeled as energy legislation and put forward by the president—with a straight face—as "not a tax" on the middle class.

As discussed in an earlier chapter, "cap and trade" essentially was proposed as a punitive tax that on paper would be levied against the largest production companies in our nation. But since the companies will simply pass along the tax increase to the consumer by raising their prices, it's the consumers who bear the brunt. Customers who are in desperate need of goods are the ones who will have no choice but to pay a higher price for necessities, and are helpless in doing anything about it. For the working poor, it can be a crippling burden. Eventually, corporations will be hurt when people can no longer afford to buy their goods.

The administration has seemed especially hostile toward the working poor. People who are trying to get themselves out of tough circumstances have been targeted to be forced into even worse circumstances—especially if they disagree. This would be largely accomplished by "card-check" legislation that President Obama promised union bosses he would personally see passed.

Essentially, card check would make it mandatory that when employees in a company vote whether or not to unionize, it would no longer be by secret ballot. Instead, everyone's vote would be public knowledge. Obama's policy direction on this matter would open up the working poor to direct harassment, threats, and even violence for the simple crime of not agreeing with the union boss.

And it's not just the administration, but also many of the president's supporters who demonstrate this contempt for the poor . . . like prominent Obama supporter Melissa Etheridge. Etheridge has joined a growing group of homosexual militants who are now threatening to withhold their taxes from the federal or state governments until what constitutes a legal marriage can be redefined so as to apply to an entire cadre of sexual unions.[1]

Since the Left constantly tell us how generous they think this nation should be by allocating the tax dollars that you and I put toward poverty relief, one would think that the personal paying of taxes would be a solid priority to them. And yet, at the first sign they won't get something to which they think they're entitled, they refuse to fund the things they say they believe in.

What liberals *really* mean is that they would prefer law-abiding people to fund government programs, but they really feel no personal compulsion to do so.

In his prime-time press conference the week of March 29, 2009, President Obama dealt dishonestly yet again with the American people. This time he was trying to justify decreasing the allowable deductions for their charitable contributions—the same contributions that have done the most good in helping the poor in America. "In that sense, what it would do is it would equalize—when I give $100, I'd get the same amount of deduction as when some—a bus driver who's making $50,000 a year, or $40,000 a year, gives that same $100. Right now, he gets 28 percent—he gets to write off 28 percent. I get to write off 39 percent. I don't think that's fair."[2]

Taxing citizens more prevents them from being able to give to charity more. And punishing taxpayers for contributing more than a certain percentage of their income is the equivalent of declaring all-out war on charitable organizations.

Any way you slice it, Obama and his ilk demonstrated contemptible disdain for the poor by suggesting changing the rules for 501(c)(3)s and merciful ministries. They did so while using them, manipulating them, and exploiting them for their own political intentions.

From purely a strategic perspective, Obama had failed even himself. There was nothing for him to fall back on. It was all on his shoulders. President Obama seemed utterly out of touch with real people. And his worthless policy priorities demonstrated that better than any opposing strategist could ever devise.

And who were left holding the bag? The poor, the unemployed, the underemployed . . .

So what *should* he have done?

TIME FOR A BIT OF CLARITY

Unlike many who exist in the pundit space of America's greatest debates today, I do desperately believe there are correct answers to the biggest challenges facing us. When I speak at worldview conferences each summer, I particularly enjoy seeing the young college-age and high school minds come alive as I put them through rounds and rounds of problem solving, some of which are on the issue of poverty. And it was only a few years ago when clarity on this issue struck me cold in the dead of night: *punishing the wealthy always hurts the poor.*

Most Americans today who are classified as "wealthy" are in fact small-business owners. They happen to bring in somewhere between $150,000 and $250,000 in total revenue. That's before they pay their employees, send in their taxes, pay their businesses' leases or mortgages, and purchase equipment, licenses, insurance, etc. What they bring home is whatever's left over after all those expenses.

When prices are low, goods are plentiful, supply chains are active, and spending is optimistic, small-business owners can thrive. And in their thriving they seldom shrink or stagnate. In fact, it is just the opposite. They look to expand, to grow, to take greater amounts of market share, and to hire more employees.

Sad to say, exactly the opposite happens when the economy begins to shrink: owners put arms around cash and don't let go; managers have to trim budgets, people are let go, unemployment begins to increase, and the solution that is needed is now hidden. Millions of people who were gainfully employed then find themselves "poor."

When this goes on long enough, it creates desperation and robs the human spirit of natural incentives toward success.

Taxation is a power of moral authority to take capital from those who produce. And it should, even must, be used gently. In America this is especially true on all taxes that affect small businesses. Small businesses create two out of three new jobs created and cannot be dealt with punitively without adversely affecting the job creation of the nation. (Which is also a moral scenario.)

What's the government's normal answer? Raise taxes . . . leading to inflation . . . leading to little or no options for small business owners. Taxes are taking something away from one person by force (and if you don't believe that, just try not paying your taxes for a few years), and giving it to someone else. That system does not create compassion, empathy, kindness, or love.

Such raw theft creates resentment, anxiety, doubt, and anger, both toward the one taking it by force and the one being given the unlawful redistributed item. But such random and unsophisticated theft also robs the one who gains the item, of independence, creativity, entrepreneurism, productivity, and ultimately success. This form of bigotry is perhaps the most evil of all. To institutionalize the belief that it is okay to believe that others are incapable of improving their circumstances through the gifts, talents, and abilities bestowed upon them by their Creator is an insidious evil.

Yet it is one this administration has felt necessary to embrace, champion, and declare.

CHAPTER FOUR

Opposing Business and Workers

In some ways, the greatest economic damage the Obama administration has inflicted on American life has been done by injuring business in general, and small business specifically. They have done so while trying to give the appearance that the disillusioned and disenfranchised are gullible enough to buy the sloganeering that government is there to protect the people.

In reality the Obama administration, from day one, launched an all-out assault on the very heart and hub of economic development in our nation. In fact, the only sector of our economy with improved employment numbers eighteen months into the president's term was the government itself. Complete with its excesses, lack of accountability, and refusal to limit its own appetite for enormous spending, the public sector added hundreds of thousands of jobs early into the "economic recovery."[1]

The private sector not only failed to mirror that growth, but in fact shrank in the opposite direction. Pledging just after inauguration that unemployment would "top out" at just under 8 percent, the Obama administration has not again seen 8 percent in general unemployment. Under George W. Bush "underemployment" (the number of families not earning enough to pay their bills, but working in the marketplace as opposed to taking unemployment benefits) was roughly one family in twenty. Under Barack Obama that number has averaged one family in five.[2]

It is this open attack on the income earners and their right to keep what they have labored for that has caused so many across the nation to sit up and take notice of issues they may have never thought much about before. In this context, small business has become preeminent in the American taxpayers' minds.

In a previous chapter we covered a little gem of a truth that I have repeated for years now: businesses don't pay taxes. When businesses are charged a tax, they absorb it by adding it to the cost of whatever they produce. The consumer who purchases their product, service, or concept is then the one left paying the amount owed to the government. So any tax increase on small business is a direct economic attack on consumers.

This truth about business is one of the reasons the Obama administration bristled so stoutly at what they viewed as venomous invective against the overhaul of the health care system. So much so that they attempted to thwart free speech. The administration encouraged those who wanted the "free health care" to intimidate those who said it was foolish to increase the tax burden upon "We the People" in the effort to "fix health care" . . .

FLAG@WHITEHOUSE.GOV

So what did the White House tell supporters to do when they ran across those who spread "disinformation" about the Obama administration's new attempt to install the anticompetitive practices of a "public option" into a federalized universal health care initiative?

Report them.

The executive branch of the federal government, in late 2009, asked you to make them aware of this "disinformation," whether it was communicated through e-mail, Web sites, blogs, or even casual conversation, because they were unable to keep track of all of the dissenters themselves. From the White House's own blog entry:

> There is a lot of disinformation about health insurance reform out there, spanning from control of personal finances to end of life care. These rumors often travel just below the surface via chain emails or through casual conversation. Since we can't keep track of all of them here at the White House, we're asking for your help. If you get an email or see something on the web about health insurance reform that seems fishy, send it to flag@whitehouse.gov.[3]

Pardon me for asking such an obvious question, but what concern is it to the president or his administration if private citizens have disagreements with, discussions over, and dissections of his efforts to take over the health care industry? Last time I checked, I had the constitutional right to do so.

But now he wishes to turn one citizen against another?

THE TOWN HALLS HEARD 'ROUND THE GLOBE

In August 2009, before the health care legislation passed, the members of Congress went home to their districts, and many of them held town halls. American citizens showed up in droves to ask questions about the viability of a plan that required the government to spend an additional $1 trillion. They wanted to know how it would affect their businesses and what it would do to their employer-provided policies. They wondered this especially when 85 percent of Americans were satisfied and content with the current health insurance system.

So what was the answer to good old-fashioned grass-roots voters actually being engaged with their congressional reps and U.S. senators? The White House believed it was best to intimidate and silence them, or—at the bare minimum—have other citizens report on them.

The mistake this White House continued to make, seemingly on a daily basis, was revealing what they truly think of the freedoms of the American political process. And it was easy to conclude it was not a very high opinion.

When President George W. Bush was being stalked by Cindy Sheehan (the activist mother of a Marine killed in Iraq) and antiwar group Code Pink on a daily basis, over a genuine issue of national security—the war on terror—he met with Sheehan, acknowledged her pain, and wished her well, all while respectfully disagreeing with her over the nation's foreign policy.

President Obama, by contrast, on April 15, 2009, when more than 2,800 Tea Parties first formed and held their debut gatherings (and an excess of 1.5 million people turned out), showed them the back of his hand and insisted on marginalizing those who sought his attention on the fundamental issue of his job performance. He did so by claiming at the end of the day that he had only heard "a little" about the grumbling of some groups. It would be months later when he would make a statement even more remarkable that while the Tea Party seemed to be complaining, in his opinion, "they should be thanking me." It was a sting that would come back to haunt him in 2010.

Then in August, there he was, asking you to report those who disagreed with him to his newly crafted e-mail address. Perhaps it would be different if "We the People" had felt the administration was dealing with us honestly.

All but admitting that they will have to raise taxes on the middle class, the White House daily fending off questions from Fox News' Major Garrett, and ABC News' Jake Tapper refusing to let the questions rest—coupled with videos of people such as Barney Frank, Jan Schakowsky, and President Obama expressing the desire for a "public option" to lead to a single payer system—gave the nation little confidence that what the administration said in prime-time press conferences was genuine.

So what should our response be? Greater demands for free speech. Louder volumes at town hall meetings. Stronger resistance the tighter they squeeze. In short, when free speech is threatened, screeching screams of volition are the only thing preventing the chokehold of silence.

So go ahead . . . report me; report us all. We will shout louder!

TAKING A PERFORMANCE REVIEW

One year after President Obama's historic election, I sized up his record, and to be honest, it was not very impressive.

Economically speaking, Obama's policies had accomplished nothing of real importance to the private sector of the American economy. In this lack of accomplishment, he had broken a string of promises. He also had advocated on behalf of policies that had taken the country into worse circumstances than when he took office. And it is arguably believable that had he done nothing but just vote "present," as he did so often in his past, the economy might have actually been in better shape.[4]

President Obama's fundamental problem was and continues to be the lack of job creation. He had pretended that such a thing as "jobs saved" by the stimulus bill money was some sort of real, tangible element that could be measured. Given that there was and is no legitimate way the number of "jobs saved" can be counted, we need to understand that this tactic was designed to throw us off the trail and to ask us to believe an unbelievable idea: that a recovery could happen without job creation.

Every president who preceded President Obama had to face the music on jobs. He refused to.

We can track other elements within the jobs sector to see if his policies are working. When the full-blown unemployment number is more than 10 percent, we get one piece of the picture. But when we add in the fact that nearly double that number of Americans have settled for underemployment, and are thus unable to truly provide completely for the needs of their families, we see the fuller picture. And the picture is officially thus: job creation and the correction of the economy were not top priorities on the president's agenda.

Two significant promises have been broken by the administration on the issue of jobs:

1. That they would prevent unemployment from ever breaching the 8 percent barrier.
2. That 90 percent of the new jobs created by the Recovery Act (aka the Stimulus) would be private sector–based jobs.

Unemployment was headed past 8 percent almost the minute that President Obama made that first promise, and the watershed of reports on the actual jobs created by the stimulus show that more than 60 percent of the jobs created thus far are in education and other public-sector entities. Hundreds of thousands of them went to public school teachers in California that were not even considered jobs in jeopardy. The reports also displayed a huge cost.

Assuming the White House's numbers are accurate (of which I have no confidence whatsoever), the $1.6 billion portion of the stimulus-allocated funds created 1 million jobs at the rate of $160,000 per job. Since roughly one-third of those jobs were in the state of California in the public education sector, and the average salary for those jobs runs $38,000 per year, how is any of this a savings? How is any of it efficient? How does any of it begin to correct problems in the larger sectors of society?

It didn't in 2009 and 2010, and it doesn't now. A year into his term, his economic grade was a D-, and that is probably more of a curve than he deserved. Today, I can't say his grade has improved any. Additional tax burdens, wasteful use of stimulus funds, and merely creating more government control are exactly the opposite of what an administration should do when needing to create more jobs. Tax reductions, especially through incentives for small businesses who hire, reduction of government spending, and relinquishing government control over the individual would be all the small businesses of America need to work our nation out of the lagging current economic hardship.

These solutions are tried and tested, they've worked in Democratic and Republican administrations in the past, and they are exactly the solutions needed today. Mr. Obama could turn the corner on his own agenda and begin to actually help the people of the United States.

But by being willing to force his agenda on the American people through very un-"hope and changey" means, Mr. Obama used his place of power to win the votes he needed on things he should not have been allowed to get. And it boiled down to one central reason . . .

Because he could!

WINDY CITY GHETTO MUSCLE: JUST "TAKING CARE OF BUSINESS!"

In the city of Chicago, "politics" is done very differently than in much of the rest of the nation. Evidently tired of hearing from "We the People," the current administration early on in its first two years seemed to demonstrate a political death wish. Many of the prominent Capitol Hill leaders seem determined to join Obama and company as they plummeted fully another sixth of the American economy into the eternal abyss. But the nation would not have arrived at that reality if President Obama had not broken very specific promises.

Most specifically he has broken his constant pledges from the campaign trail to be a different kind of leader. He pledged to be a leader who listened to those who elected him. He even pledged on the night he won the vote to listen to those who opposed him.[5] Yet in the final week leading up to the vote on health care reform, he was listening to no one, and doing so at our great peril.

Voices from the center, left, and right had barraged their senators' offices, indicating their displeasure with the lack of transparency in the process (meeting in closed-room sessions) and substance (the bill had not even been fully written and the senators knew "enough" to vote on it) of the health care legislation. Yet it was Obama's iron fist, his nasty scowl, and his hard-core Chicago bullying that was most interestingly revealed the week before the vote.

President Obama was willing to play games with America's safety in threatening Nebraska's Ben Nelson that a strategic and vital military base, one responsible for heavy lifting on America's continental security, would be shut down if Nelson did not vote with him. President Obama was going to put a bullet in the operations of our national security simply to score a point, serve a little vengeance, and punish with a little payback. We know this, and we also know that it wasn't the only time in recent history that such tactics have been employed by Obama.[6]

Congressional Democrats stepped forward that same week, fessing up that they had felt compelled to vote with the president's legislation. The administration had informed them that it would be watching—and "keeping score" (the specific words of Rahm Emanuel, the White House chief of staff). In a very real sense, this is exactly what Obama was doing to the nation as a whole.

There was no majority of American people that believed this bill was sound or helpful or would bring down costs. And we later learned from the Congressional Budget Office that earliest estimates indicated they would go up significantly.

Even with all the problems of the uninsured walking into emergency rooms, America provides health services to everyone within its borders. The cost of how we do it now was roughly $1.3 trillion per year, by Congressional sources. According to those same actuaries and auditories, the cost of Obamacare is conservatively estimated at tipping $4 trillion per year—to cover the exact same number of people.

Obama's pride had been injured greatly throughout the year. He had failed at nearly everything possible in office, except exporting our tax dollars to pay for abortions overseas—that he did swiftly. His Olympic, Nobel, and global warming endeavors all verged on the utterly ridiculous, and the man's pride was hurt. If he did not accomplish health care reform before Congress adjourned that year, he would have gone one full year without any significant accomplishment. Gitmo was still open; soldiers were still in Iraq; more were headed to Afghanistan. His pledge to produce a healed economy and a better jobs picture was equally laughable in that he'd made both worse. At the time of final passage of the health care reform legislation fight, forty-nine out of fifty states had *lost* jobs since the stimulus was passed.

In Copenhagen that same week, he lashed out at China, and got made fun of by the only new allies he'd made in office. Fidel Castro, one of his heroes, called him "ignorant," and Hugo Chavez said he still smelled of Satanic sulfur (a reference with which he had previously only regaled President Bush).

Then, when poll after poll across America demonstrated that two-thirds of the American people were solidly against Obamacare, the president was ready to jam it down Americans' throats. But it is crucial for our own sake that President Obama remembers that he's not a Chicago mob boss; he works for us.

TIME FOR A BIT OF CLARITY

It is important to clarify that President Obama is not the first, nor do I suspect he will be the last, president to pit business against government in an attempt to pitch the debate as the evil executive versus the good public servant. But he and any future presidents who choose to, do it at our peril, especially if we allow them to get away with it. Bullying tactics, whether they stem from snitch programs encouraging you to report on your neighbors, or buying off or threatening political damage to Congressional members, cannot be countenenced.

But the truth is, rather than doing the very thing that would stimulate an economic growth spurt—court the nation's small businesses, wildly feed their enthusiasm, and help them grow—the administration went in the opposite direction. Based on a ruthlessly pragmatic hunch, they believed that giving out "free" health care would benefit them long past when America would lift herself out of the recessionary doldrums.

Vital to our understanding of the future, for the welfare of everyone who will listen, is this: We can't wait for others to watch, sheriff, pay attention, and act. We must, in a sense, become the change we want to see.

I know, I know; I know it's a line directly from Obama, but it's a good line. The difference is, *we* must apply it with honest, sound principle, and be vigilant in our ruthless pursuit of truth!

CHAPTER FIVE

Risky Business
Empowering People to
Economic Freedom

One of the big differences between an Obama economy and the economy of John F. Kennedy or Ronald Reagan is the central importance of what causes economic growth. As the economy progressed under the guidance of Obama policies, one thing became increasingly clear: the administration was either fearful or ignorant about the single most important element needed for economic health, not to mention long-term recovery.

That element is risk.

Without risk, and even more important, the entrepreneurial "risk takers," enterprise, employment, production, and quality of life all begin to sag. This is true from the corner store to the Wall Street firm. Risk stimulates growth. While risk isn't the perfect answer to every problem in a financially based society, it solves more problems than it leaves, and in the end even risks that have turned out poorly can benefit society, because they give birth to reinvention.

President Obama knows there are two sides to allowing risk into a free market. He has used both sides of the argument to argue his policies. Without risk a society's economic growth is stifled. People "settle." Potential entrepreneurs give up on dreams, goals, and ambitions to own their own business—and these are the very lifeblood of any healthy economy in American history.

President Obama, for all of the negative possibilities, is exceedingly averse to risk. He likes outcome guarantees. He would like to be able to guarantee that neighbor A makes the same exact amount of money through full-time work as neighbor B. Never mind the fact that neighbor A works only four hours a day and refuses to look for additional opportunity, while neighbor B built a business with his own sweat equity over thirty years, working eighteen hours a day.

What President Obama seeks is equal outcomes, not equal opportunity to succeed.

We saw this in significant ways in the early Obama administration takeover of banks and car companies. Other private-sector entities had control of their operations subverted to federal whims. But most important, takeovers rubbed out the element of risk and all the fruit that would have benefited the economic stability of a nation as a result.

Risk can be harmful for some. Refusing to allow risk in society as a whole is always harmful, for far many more. In the Obama White House, this anti-risk mentality set in very early in the administration.

ECONOMIC ELASTICITY IS GOOD

President Obama had dug himself into an even deeper hole than had been expected in his attempt to deliver on key campaign promises. In the days in February and March 2009 alone (the first two months solely on his watch), he presided over a record-breaking increase in unemployment, with nearly 2 million additional unemployed persons than when he took office. The national unemployment rate now surged well past 8.5 percent (double that of the average of George W. Bush's two terms), Obama's unemployment percentage quickly shot to the highest in twenty-five years, and his total of unemployed persons drawing benefits from the government sat at more than 13 million gross. That exceeded the 11 million-plus of the Great Depression era.

If President Obama inherited "the greatest recession since the Great Depression,"—a quote from nearly every campaign speech Barack Obama made while running for president in 2008—then his policies, lack of action, and wrongheaded decisions surged the nation beyond it. In pointing this out, a commenter on my blog in the early weeks of 2009 chided me: "It might take more than seventy-two days to fix it." No one doubted that. But we were still only seeing the tip of the iceberg in terms of where his *Titanic*-type view of the economy was leading us.

You only need to understand a single word to grasp the full concept: *elasticity.* It is what Obama's policies lack, and without it there will be no economic recovery for some time. Obama's trends in unemployment, consumer confidence, and economic recovery will stagnate—and that isn't going to help anyone.

Elastic "conditions" (federal tax policies) encourage business owners, patent holders, and idea generators to engage in risk, set up companies, hire people, and attempt to create, produce, or distribute goods and services. The economic elasticity comes in the form of sacrifice in which the individual idea generator, patent holder, or business owner is willing to engage. Some of these visionaries will mortgage their homes, sell off all their goods, and risk everything on the confidence of their ideas. Understanding that the onus of their success rests upon their own shoulders, they engage in the level of risk or sacrifice with which they are comfortable, in the hopes of producing far more than what they originally put at risk in the first place.

Risk is the currency in an elastic economy. It says to someone who has an idea for a product, "Do you think you can actually pull this thing off?"

Traditionally in economies where America has thrived, we have made it our business as a society to reward those who take the risk. We do this through tax incentives for invention, business development, hiring workers, and increasing production.

So if the federal government recognized, for example, that new inventions might make production of goods or services in our society more efficient, then they could give that particular effort (or more specifically, the people who were engaged in that effort) a lower tax burden for that calendar year.

Since the unemployment numbers have dogged us so horrifically since Obama came to office, giving incentives to companies who truly focus on product development and growth of their reach would make tremendous financial sense. And the same could be argued for hiring more workers, or producing products in even greater abundance.

And why not? If a government is willing to attach a tax on anything they can get 51 percent of Congress to vote in favor of, why can't we be just as freely willing to reduce taxes on efforts that genuinely drive economic stimulation? And I'm not referring to silly temporary policies of single-issue tax credits for hiring, but rather, long-term tax relief that grows a company's bottom line without fear of the government taking more from the operational kitty.

Engaging in risk does not benefit everyone who dares, and many lessons have been learned by society and the individuals who have failed. But it is resolutely true that without many risk takers undergoing the lumps in their throats, the sinking in the pit of their stomachs, and the massive sacrifice of much, the American economy would have dried up long ago.

The problems with Obama's entire approach to economic development is that he replaces risk with status quo, limited outcomes, and static conditions for all. For what it's worth, static conditions do exactly the opposite of risk. People, especially those who have capital to spend, become rigid, tight, and unbending with their money.

I was with a CEO of a company in Virginia (several, actually) in the spring of 2009. In the middle of breakfast, one of the CEOs blurted out across the table to Governor Mike Huckabee, who was also with us, "When conditions are bad, get your arms around the cash." In other words, hold on to resources, become miserly, take less risk, and attempt less or even no growth. When risk is looked at as suspect, success is punished as criminal, and taxes force the productive to no longer be motivated to achieve more, things generally tend to grind to a painfully ugly halt. And that's exactly where we found ourselves in 2009.

Elastic economies create, produce, thrive, and teach lessons. Static ones stunt, inhibit, block, and eventually shut down.

TIME FOR A BIT OF CLARITY

Risk does one other thing that is truly important for us to understand as we move into the economy of the second decade of the new century—it holds us accountable to ourselves.

Risk is ultimately a test between what people think of themselves and what they believe they can achieve. One of the reasons America was great from its beginning was the belief that we could conquer a previously unconquered land, that if we allowed individuals the opportunity to choose for themselves the type of life they wished for, they could create it. And that if we removed the blockage of government and other types of burdens and intrusions upon the worker, he would lead a better life because he would want the best life possible.

This is *still* the reason why so many risk life and limb crossing perilous waters from Cuba or Haiti to attempt to get into the United States. In large measure, the opportunity to "make something of one's life" is the biggest problem we have related to illegal immigration.

Like it or not, America is perceived as a place where you are allowed to risk it all, for a payout that's even bigger—if you work hard in the interim. It is this very element that the Obama administration should be seeking to encourage *more* of, not less, if we are to have a brighter economic vision for our future.

CHAPTER SIX

Rush Wanted Obama to Fail; Obama Wants America to Fail

When America's most listened-to talk show host first proclaimed it, the predictable occurred. Mainstream networks asked tons of Republican politicians if they agreed with Rush Limbaugh's statement, and most of them decidedly did not. The rather casual comment Limbaugh made in the opening weeks of Obama's administration? "I hope Obama fails."[1]

Normal people, in normal contexts, under normal conditions would simply blink, think to themselves that he really had an opinion about the matter, and then go about their lives. (Which is exactly what 98 percent of America did. But the networks were apoplectic at hearing the "f" word used in conjunction with the man that most of them had vowed was the nearest thing to a human messiah the world had ever seen. "In-depth" reports were ordered, lengthy editorials were written, and Republicans, of course, tucked their tails between their legs and ran the other way.)

Yet Rush was merely stating a truth he had expressed a few thousand times previously. In fact, he had even expressed, when he first read my column predicting that Obama would become president, that a presidency containing the policies on which Obama was campaigning would be exceedingly bad for the nation. So if you rooted for America's success, you had to, by necessity, hope that either Obama abandoned those policies, or that they failed.

And ironically, President Obama and his team needed the nations to experience some failure in order to feed their own selfish ambition.

CHEERING ON THE CRISIS

"Don't let a good crisis go to waste."

This idea popped up multiple times in more than seven days in early 2009 as members of Obama's administration seemed to be in total agreement. Their conclusion: by not quickly solving the crisis of the American economy, they could create drastic social and structural change. Not surprisingly, this was the very strategy President Obama alluded to in his Saturday address to the nation that week.

The president challenged his country to see its hard times as a chance to "discover great opportunity in the midst of great crisis." "That is what we can do and must do today. And I am absolutely confident that it is what we will do," Obama said in his address.[2] Use "great opportunities" to change the face and fabric of the nation? That wasn't exactly what "We the People" hired him to do.

"We the People" hired him to take swift and effective action toward getting the markets repaired—as he promised to do—but at the time of this address, the stock market had dropped about 1,400 points each week since he'd taken power.

We were promised greater fiscal responsibility by candidate Obama, yet his own proposals threw us down a black hole of debt, the likes of which we'd never seen in a single year of an administration, much less in the first sixty days of one.

We were promised the greatest commitment ever to oversight of the federal use of the money we send the government. What we'd been handed was a series of embarrassing nominations of people who are willing to use the force of a gun to make you pay your taxes, but did not think twice about not paying theirs.

We were told that the president's push for a stimulus would get people working again, yet barely 3 percent of it went to actual job creation and projects that could be initiated over twenty-four months.

We were promised greater employment fulfillment and more vibrant business and economic outlooks when Obama's administration finally put together their plan to save the lending institutions. What we were left to deal with was a greater spike in the unemployment numbers in Obama's first sixty days than was experienced under President Bush in his first seven years.

And "We the People" were promised an earmark-free, pork-free, bare-bones budget; Obama's omnibus bill contained 9,200 earmarks.

So I didn't then and don't now find it surprising that even Obama supporters are now openly questioning his plan to revive the economy. We know that more than 55 percent of the American people wanted help for the economy to come primarily through tax reduction. The same poll found that only a little more than 20 percent believed greater government spending was the answer.

Whoopi Goldberg surprised even herself on *The View* that same week, unintentionally criticizing President Obama's plan to tax the American people into better economic conditions. She didn't believe that she should have to turn around and write a check to Washington, D.C., for nearly 40 percent of what she earned. Who could blame her?

Yet it is important to point out that there are now far more economists on record that have advised the president against larger government and pushed him toward tax relief than those who supported the increased centralized control of a soft socialism that President Obama seems destined to aim for. And we should be asking ourselves why.

If it makes no sense to the free-market economists that populate the best economics programs across the nation, if it weakens the ability for the average family to make ends meet, and if it does not increase the number of people actually working, why did President Obama so stubbornly continuing to pursue his economically diabolical plan of destruction?

Because it was potentially part of the master plan to "not let a good crisis go to waste."

President Obama knows the history of recessions and how Americans get out of them. He knows, for example, that if he gave back to the American family in just pure cash handouts what he had instead been planning on taxing them (with interest) in the days to come, the number would loom between $25,000 and $65,000 per family, for every family in America.

But pretending to be doing something about the problem is only half the strategy for Obama. He truly intended to see centralized government control of health care, and European-style labor agreements become reality in America. He knew the consequences of doing such things; he'd seen all the projections and what the outcomes would be, but he did it anyway.

But there is one tiny problem standing in his way: "We the People"!

He knows that forcing us down paths that we don't wish to take will create abject suffering and misery. Then he can promise to take America to a better place economically, a place of greater care, a place of true serenity. A place like Venezuela.

While discussing Limbaugh's desire for the president to fail, Rachel Maddow, host on MSNBC and former morning drive personality on Air America Radio, told Jay Leno that same week that she found it "creepy" that someone would want the president's policies to fail.[3] I found it disturbing that Rachel Maddow was so ignorant that she refused to think analytically concerning her president's plan for this nation. After all she is one of us "We the People."

President Obama and his team did not intend to solve the economic crisis as quickly as they possibly could—as he had previously promised on the campaign trail. Instead, his intention was to let us bleed until the whimper builds into an all-out, gut-wrenching cry of anguish. He did not care what had to be done to arrive at that reality, only that we arrived there.

Many think the Obama administration is incompetent, and surely they've proved this, from the vetting of their appointments to handling the limited foreign relationships they've entertained thus far. But on the domestic agenda they are as sly as foxes, and our future is the henhouse.

And in refusing to allow a "good crisis" to go to waste, the strategic move to remake America anew had just begun . . .

THE SIGNS WERE EVERYWHERE

"Never has an administration who had more firepower at their disposal, been set to so totally fail in the next six to eight weeks."

Thus began my contributer's column for Fox News, published September 1, 2009, "Why the Obama Administration Will Implode in Weeks."[4] In nearly every box the president had come into office hoping to put a check mark, dismal failure was pretty much the only option listed.

That would change . . . in so many ways.

Most significantly, on Christmas Eve the Senate would "deem passed" the greatest overhaul in the history of legislation. They would do so with 74 percent of the American people staring them in the face, telling them not to, but they did it anyway. That health care reform bill outcome, however, only reinforced the assertions I made in the piece for Fox, which went on to become the single most-read piece in the history of Fox News. It was nearly a foregone conclusion. Implosion was almost unavoidable. And it defied all logic, given the sizable majority the administration had in both houses of Congress.

Those next few weeks, I believed, would take the administration down a course that would effectively halt the radical transformation that appeared unstoppable only months previous. I based the entire premise on six reasons:

1. **Health care had suffered a long and painful death.** I said at the time, "Barring the existing possibility that the Democrats cram a reform bill down the throats of actively protesting Americans through an ultra-partisan process that would shut out conservatives and Republicans from even being allowed to contribute to the discussion, health care reform is dead."[5] (Never had a more accurate prediction of how the process would take place been uttered.) But health care *had* died; at least the version that the president most desperately wanted had. It had actually died a good while before, when the president decided to pivot and create a new issue that no one had been discussing—health insurance reform. "The American people," I proffered, "will want to know why we should spend $4 billion to cover everyone in America 'efficiently,' when we already do so with inefficiencies like people using the emergency room as their general practitioner for $2.5 billion."[6] Deep thinkers on the issue wanted to know why the president hadn't entertained one item of tort reform—protecting his friends, the trial lawyers—yet had been willing to claim that doctors were eager to lop off feet, tonsils, and foreskins just to make a buck.

2. **Cap and trade would be the largest tax increase in American history.** With the 2010 election cycle just around the corner, campaign ads were not far off from being drafted. Cap and trade was still sitting in legislative limbo, and the president's own adviser—Warren Buffet—took to opposing it openly in the media. The "9-12 Project" was in the works, which resulted in the largest gathering of anti-tax Americans coming to Washington, D.C. The Blue Dog Democrats who supported cap and trade were getting absolutely hammered in their home districts. It seemed as though another single-party ram-through victory on the matter would not be wise.

   Cap and trade, if passed at some point in the future, will still contribute to unemployment, Wall Street stops and starts, and ultimately, reduced Treasury revenues. It would serve as the single largest tax increase on the average American in all of U.S. history. Even President Obama admitted as much, predicting that electric bills, in his words, would "skyrocket."[7] Those in the Congressional Budget Office, who had looked at the specifics, tell us that the average utility bill in America will go from $167 to $307 per month, per family.

3. **Unemployment would remain high.** Several Washington organizations from left and right, and one of note consisting of both—the Congressional Budget Office—began to predict that unemployment was not going to shrink anytime soon from the predicted "Obama high" of 8 percent. Instead, nearly without fail, economists began predicting unemployment at or over 10 percent for up to the next twenty-four months. That was nearly a 250 percent increase over the numbers we saw under Bush for nearly the duration of his two-term presidency. If people were working, higher taxes and possible new health care entitlements could be considered, but without them working it would be political suicide for Democrats. And the debates around the November 2010 elections were off and running.

4. **Obama's integrity was tarnished as early as August of year 1.** Not a great deal had been made of the whoppers that the president had been telling while the federal government was in recess in the summer of 2009. Still, it is worth noting that many more people than I had previously realized had noticed the president "exaggerating" badly in his talks on health care—for instance, confusing the actual amount physicians got to amputate a foot ($500) with the $50,000 that he claimed they got. He began to show an utter disregard for the reputations of those about whom he spoke, the "facts" he used to make his argument, and his overly optimistic views about the results of his policies. At the beginning of summer 2009, Americans mostly trusted him; his passion index was at +10 in the Rasmussen daily tracking poll, but he went into his freshman fall at –14.

5. **A $3 trillion budget**. This was the actual budget for the fiscal year 2009. This was in addition to the $750 billion in bailout spending that had already taken place. "New spending" for this and that sure added up. And that brought me to number 6.

6. **A looming middle-class tax hike**. The president's supporters would hem and haw. Official lip service was given, often from the ever-arrogant White House press secretary, Robert Gibbs, to being "good stewards" and to being a "responsible administration" that "pays as it goes." But the truth was then and still is, in order to pay for everything they've promised and budgeted for, a tax increase loomed for small businesses and working families that President Obama promised would never come. And as an aside, he was going to break that promise all along. Because the minute the "Bush tax relief" ran out in 2010, middle-class taxes would be going up in an "Obama administration." Hence, fundamentally, Obama's "not a single dime" pledge on the campaign trail was a lie from start to finish. Ironically the deal that President Obama cut with Republicans in the closing hours of 2010 merely delayed his desire to raise taxes. But fundamentally did not change his desire to eventually see them evaporate.

Of course, the president, the Democrats, the Left, and Congressional leadership could've surprised me. They could've shown up in September 2009, endorsed the Coburn-Ryan proposed health care bill (a solid and fiscally responsible health care bill offered by the Republicans) in the U.S. Senate, and swiped the credit for it. They could've shown up the next week and fought with all their might to not allow the tax rates to skyrocket in 2010. They could've decided to scrap cap and trade and rethink the use of public money for true job-based economic stimulation. But I didn't hold my breath, and I advised others against it as well.

What the administration *did* do was awaken the American worker, the American small-business owner, and the American voter, all three of whom began wondering aloud, "What on earth have we done?"

BUT WHAT ABOUT THE BEER?

President Barack Obama developed a tendency early in his administration to stick himself in the middle of conflicts that were of essentially no concern to the chief executive's office, like the incident between the Cambridge Massachusetts police and a Harvard lecturer, where the white police officer was accused of racism for arresting a black professor. Obama started by proclaiming that the officer had acted "stupidly," and ended by inviting the two men to the White House for a beer in an effort to ease the racial tensions the whole thing caused.

In my opinion he owed a different issue the courtesy of his involvement. In understanding the vital importance of genuine issues of equality in a postracial (aka "Obamian") age, he owed it to the NFL, DeMaurice Smith, Donovan McNabb, Jennifer Lopez, Serena Williams, Fergie, and Ja Rule to invite them, along with Rush Limbaugh, to come enjoy a beer on the White House lawn with him and his vice president. Of course, given Joe Biden's history of racist statements toward Indians, Pakistanis, and even Obama, perhaps even the VP could learn a thing or two.

Rush Limbaugh had been black-balled from becoming a part owner in an NFL franchise, mostly because he was Rush Limbaugh. Astoundingly, Obama remained silent on the matter.

The difference between the "beer summit" and this one might be the fact that President Obama just might have had to say some not-so-nice things to some of those gathered around the table. Also, once it was revealed that the primary force behind the attack on Rush Limbaugh was in fact a former Obama campaign aide and now a high-ranking official with the NFL Player's Association, named DeMaurice Smith, the president would necessarily be forced to disassociate himself from him à la William Ayers and Jeremiah Wright.

But one topic of conversation that would actually be helpful to everyone watching would be: "Why are openly racist, divisive, and vulgar people allowed to be owners in the NFL, while a man who has no history of racism whatsoever is prevented from it?" Obama's a law professor, and law professors love those kinds of questions.

But for the sake of argument, let's be more specific (per Brietbart's Big Hollywood): why was Jennifer Lopez allowed to be a minority owner in the NFL (Miami Dolphins) when she has used the "n" word in reference to football players? Actually, what she said was a lot worse, but my editor won't let me print it. You can look up the lyrics she penned for her song called "I'm Real" if you're that interested. Lopez had actually uttered those words hundreds of times, in front of thousands of people and their kids. "Mega Producer" Ja Rule helped her record the song, performed in her video, and the two have taken the show in front of actual live audiences. Lopez was part of an entire cadre of celebrity minority owners for the Miami Dolphins, and they pretty much all have mouths their mothers wouldn't kiss.

Serena Williams, also a minority NFL owner (again Dolphins), dropped dozens of "F-bombs" in a partially race-based tirade in her most embarrassing moment at the U.S. Open in 2009, breaking several FCC laws in the process as well.

Limbaugh had been labeled as divisive, yet "musical" artist "Fergie" (minority owner for the Dolphins) sang a song about the real reason for the Iraq war being swept under the rug by the CIA. She repeated these lyrics in front of thousands of people as part of her stint as a Black-Eyed Pea going back all the way to 2003. Perhaps, though, when you're a huge Obama supporter like Fergie, you can be as offensive as you wish, with no repercussions whatsoever. She sang the song "Glamorous" at the White House for Easter—you know, the day Christ rose from the dead? Suffice it to say that any lyrics that contain the phrase "take your broke a— home" are probably not appropriate for the Easter crowd.

Meanwhile, what was Rush Limbaugh's great crime against humanity, race, and decency? He simply stated in 2003 that Donovan McNabb has been given extra-sensitive treatment by coaches over the years because of his role as one of the few black quarterbacks in the NFL: "I don't think he's been that good from the get-go. I think what we've had here is a little social concern in the NFL. I think the media has been very desirous that a black quarterback do well . . . I think there's a little hope invested in McNabb and he got a lot of credit for the performance of his team that he really didn't deserve. The defense carried this team."[8]

This statement was not only factually true; it had been easily provable over the years.

When word became public in 2009 that Limbaugh wished to purchase a stake in an NFL team, the cries of racism reared their ugly heads again. In defense of Rush, some prominent retired NFL players—who happen to be African-American—as well as even liberal African-American pundits stated openly that the attack by Obama operatives inside the NFL to kill Rush's chances at ownership were the only racist actions in this entire sad affair. And their strong feeling was that doing such damage to Rush would hinder free speech for conservatives across the board.

By way of response, Warren Ballantine and others from the militantly angry within the black community let loose with commands to return to "the porch." It was a clearly racist and degrading command, made even more intense by the use of it from one black man to another.

President Obama's election was supposed to be historical because it represented the truth that though there are racist people in America even today, the plague of racism will never again prevent a black man from rising to highest capacity of achievement. But regrettably, it seemed the most disturbing form of discrimination appeared to be meted out for those who opposed the policies of that same man. And isn't that ironic given the fact that criticism from those who oppose him should be the loudest proof of total equality?

Had Mr. President had the courage that he pretended to, given his supposed convictions, he could've cleared all this up. Perhaps it was easier to just buy the next round . . .

But despite missing out on the opportunity to have a beer summit for Rush Limbaugh and the NFL, Mr. Obama does stay focused on getting his agenda passed. Like the made-for-TV stuff.

"AND NOW, FROM HEALTH CARE CENTRAL . . ."

When President Obama concluded a seven-hour, made-for-television faux summit on health reform, and more or less announced his intention to cram his signature bill through the Senate in the form of a "reconciliation bill," he sealed his choice in moving forward with a great wager. The reconciliation process is designed to be used *only* for budget bills in the Congress. This is a bet that he was hedging to see if the electorate would be more forgiving of him once he'd be able to claim that he'd accomplished something—anything—in his first two years in office. As I was the first person in American punditry to predict this president's success to elected office, let me again go out on the prediction limb to say on this, "He will fail." I'm basing my gut feeling on two polls released by a news organization. And nope, it's not Fox News. It's CNN!

The CNN/Opinion Research poll released August 2, 2009, was the first shocking poll. Only 25 percent of Americans wanted either of the Obamacare bills to be passed and turned into law.

The Republicans attempted to point this out to the president, the vice president, the Speaker of the House, and the Senate majority leader. They attempted to point it out to the minority leader and to the remainder of the Democrats gathered who were supposedly called there to the faux summit to "listen" to the Republicans share their health care ideas. I say "supposedly" listen because the Republicans were given less than two full hours out of the event's seven and a half to actually speak. Maybe it's just me, but five and a half hours for one side and one hour and fifty-four minutes for the other doesn't seem like much "listening."

The CNN poll also showed that 48 percent of Americans wished the president and Congress would scrap the current bills and start the discussion and process on health care reform all over again, something else senators Lamar Alexander and Tom Coburn were particularly skilled at pointing out. The Democrats, however, acted as though they could not hear them.

The same CNN poll showed that another 25 percent of Americans wished the federal government would drop health care reform for the time being—altogether. My hunch is that these are folks who believe, like most of us, that if you fix the jobs problem, then more people will automatically get health care.

Since it was unlikely that the jobs numbers were to change anytime soon, the president chose to double down and go for the jugular on health care. In a sense, he'd sort of backed into a corner. He hadn't improved the economy; the unemployment situation had still not stabilized and was, in fact, worse; Gitmo was still open; six terrorist attacks against the U.S. had happened on his watch; and people were tired of all of his speeches while seeing no results.

He'd also created another monumental issue that he would have a hard time overcoming: According to another CNN/Opinion Research poll, a majority of Americans now felt that the government could not be trusted. Specifically, 56 percent of the American people believed the government was intruding upon the basic rights of its citizens, or so they said in December 2009. The survey showed that 4 in 10 Democrats felt that way, as well as 6 in 10 Independents.

The entire debate surrounding the cronyism of the stimulus bills, the takeover of private enterprise in the bailout programs, the usurpation of the free market on the health care debate, and the desire to raise the most punitive taxes against consumers ever imagined in the cap-and-trade legislation all were contributors to this feeling. The youth vote, which gave Obama his 4 percent win in the electorate (beating McCain by 40 percent in the demographic), felt this "intrusion" effect most acutely.

The American people were telling CNN, not Fox News, that they did not like the president's priorities or his policies. The young Americans who were being asked to shoulder these nightmarish realities in their future were agitated. And American voters were more aware of the legislative score than Obama was letting on.

So, since President Obama and his Democratic Senate leadership pushed the misapplied process of "reconciliation" to pass a bill that 75 percent of the nation did not want, just to get it through the Senate, what would his trick be when he got it in front of the House, where Nancy Pelosi was then twenty-one votes short of passage?

They would outright buy the votes. Threatening the removal of an air base in one senator's district (see chapter 4), cutting a deal with a senator in Louisiana, and the infamous Florida perks promised in the "gator-raid" discussions were just some of the memorable examples. Promising stimulus dollars in some districts, they even got a group of supposedly pro-life Democrats to vote against their conscience and ultimately pass a bill that had gaping loopholes for offering taxpayer-funded abortions.

The American people were watching, they didn't like it, and most important—similar to Mr. Limbaugh—we the people began wishing Obama's policies would fail.

TIME FOR A BIT OF CLARITY

It was not an arguable or even disagreeable proposition when Rush Limbaugh announced his desire for the newly minted president's policies to fail. It was simply the truth as Limbaugh saw it, no matter who in the media disagreed with him and called him a racist. Being agreeable to things that should be disagreed with is far more foolish than rooting for the failure of horrible ideas.

I say it on my radio show nonstop: "Clarity is *always* preferable to unity!"

To fully understand our government's policies, our candidates' desires, and the outcomes of their efforts should be paramount to all else when deciding who we are choosing to vote for. Yet people make a mockery of this process because of a false belief that non-criticism somehow leads to enlightenment. It *never* does. It never can. It never will. The reverse is far more true: questioning, probing, digging, and thinking are far likelier to yield better results in nearly every area of life.

It starts with getting better information and having greater interest in how policy is made. It continues with how we incorporate personal principles into the lives of our children and others we influence. And ultimately the greatest fruit that can be evidenced from it is in how our families, communities, churches, and nation change as a result of it.

Unity around silliness breeds an unbearable society. That's why we must first understand what we are supposedly agreeing with, and when necessary, we should root for the ideas that oppose wisdom to, in a word . . .

Fail.

PART TWO

"National Insecurity"

CHAPTER
SEVEN

Obama's America "Unlike Anything We've Ever Known"

Election night, November 5, 2008: A packed house had filled Grant Park on Chicago's lakefront. The venue normally used for jazz festivals, Shakespeare performances, and rallies for victorious World Champions was crowded with people there for another type of victory. Chicago's very own Barack Obama had just been elected president of the United States. Though it was quite cold, even people like Jesse Jackson—who had previously promised to surgically alter Obama's manhood over comments about the responsibility black men have to their families—were huddled in winter coats, hats, and gloves, awaiting the victory speech of the attractive, young president-elect.

Obama's speech that night was heavy on the "hope and change" he had so readily invoked many times previously:

If there is anyone out there who still doubts that America is a place where all things are possible; who still wonders if the dream of our founders is alive in our time; who still questions the power of our democracy, tonight is your answer . . .

It's the answer spoken by young and old, rich and poor, Democrat and Republican, black, white, Latino, Asian, Native American, gay, straight, disabled and not disabled—Americans who *sent a message* to the world that we have never been a collection of Red States and Blue States: we are, and always will be, the United States of America . . .

It's been a long time coming, but tonight, because of what we did on this day, in this election, at this *defining moment*, change has come to America . . .

The road ahead will be long. *Our climb will be steep.* We may not get there in one year or even one term, but America—I have never been more hopeful than I am tonight that we will get there. I promise you—we as a people will get there.[1]

Though most Americans did not realize it at the time those words were spoken, the "steep climb," the "defining moment," and the "message that was sent," were intended far more explicitly than the celebration of an historic night would allow them to imagine. "Fundamental transformation," was a term in the president's inaugural address that he never shied away from using, but the electorate took it to mean something far different.

President Obama's inaugural was one for the history books. The first African-American president to take the oath of office had to have felt the pressure of the moment, of the burden of history placed on his shoulders. It's understandable that some things were going to go wrong. The oath of office wasn't said correctly—and later the same day he had to repeat the oath privately, away from the eye of the public.

Little did the nation understand that this flub would turn out to be a foreshadowing of what was to come for the nation in just weeks.

Hardly anyone knew until some days later that moments after being sworn in, the very first action that the president took in office was to immediately issue an executive order that forced millions of the nation's hard-earned tax dollars into the abortion business overseas. Yes, America quickly began to look like something that was vastly unrecognizable to most of her citizens.

But the president had told us from the beginning that change was coming, and it was his intention to make that message clear. His attempts to do so, however, were very muddled along the way.

STUMBLING OUT OF THE GATE

For roughly the first five months in office, President Obama went on media offense. To keep our national love affair with the historic president active, he kept his face and charm fresh in our minds. The president gave interviews with nearly every network, went on late-night comedy shows, asked for network airtime, and reveled in the way the media fawned over his glossy new title.

It would have probably been wiser for him to chart a different course.

On March 19, 2009, this advice would've been especially helpful. During an appearance on *The Tonight Show with Jay Leno*, Leno asked the president about his bowling score. But when Obama could have taken the opportunity to be truly self-deprecating, he instead made an off-hand joke and lambasted Special Olympians.

Here's how it went down: "No, no. I have been practicing . . . I bowled a 129. It's like—it was like Special Olympics, or something."[2] That same weekend America Online did a "Hot Seat" poll, and 84 percent of the American people, according to the results, thought the joke he cracked on late-night television was either tone-deaf/insensitive or worse yet, flat-out offensive.

He also had terrible timing. Ironically he made this comment the day before World Down Syndrome Day. I personally received e-mails, tweets, and MySpace/Facebook messages from hundreds of parents in the forty-eight hours after the president cracked the joke about Special

Olympians, some of whom could easily take President Obama in any number of sports. I heard from families who have Down syndrome children, one family who had three, a number of messages from families who had just identified their children as challenged or disabled, and some who told me that their child's diagnosis—like my own son's—was mental or physical retardation.

He does know what *retardation* means, doesn't he? Literally it means "slow." Sort of identical to the way his economic recovery plan was working.

But that was just one of more than several dozen gaffes the new president committed in this season of overexposure to the media. Britain's largest daily newspaper had a top ten gaffe reel assembled when his presidency was barely sixty days old.

He took the time to address the Iranian Islamic Republic via YouTube (after they had been burning him in effigy for weeks), with a plea to come to the table of intellects and have a philosophical wine-and-cheese night. Instead, ripples of laughter could be heard from Tehran a full five days later.

Now, if these elements composed the entire universe of faux pas he committed in his brief time in office, then he might have been able to withstand them. But he followed up these embarrassments with things like giving the prime minister of Britain twenty-five DVDs that were not even compatible with European media players. He even refused to accept priceless gifts from fellow heads of state, including one item that represented the cause of abolition and which had been fashioned from the timbers from an antique slave ship. It just began to look tacky.

And Obama was not satisfied with plastering himself on every magazine cover; he sought out the late-night spotlight in ways that make even former president Clinton look chaste, frequently interrupting prime-time television. This forced networks to lose millions of dollars in ad revenue, causing them to have to lay people off. And in his "demonstrable insecurity of needing people to like [him]" (my term at the time), he was scheduled to be back before the nation's networks just three days later . . . again!

Would that news conference be like the one he had put on the last time? Only weeks earlier he had filibustered the answering of the questions, spending a full ten minutes answering the very first one. It was at that press conference that he had promised us that his federal treasury team, led by tax evader Timothy Geitner, would present us a plan to save the banking system "the next morning!" President Obama even refused to answer a question related to the issue, citing the following morning's "plan."

The truth was, even that early in his presidency, President Obama had hundreds of economists pointing him to the proper solutions for the economy. And yet, he would not act.

Where was his plan

- to deal with a now nuclear-boasting Iran?
- to deal with a growing nuclear capability in North Korea?
- to halt the job losses in nearly a dozen states that were hovering near 10 percent unemployment (more than double the national average of Bush's entire two terms)?
- to create opportunity for risk takers to create new business or start new companies that could hire people and put them to work?

He had made time to publicly select NCAA picks for the 2009 March Madness. But the truth was, most of the nation thought that a basketball coach at Duke was more qualified for his job than he was.

One of his closest advisers and longest supporters, Warren Buffet, recently stated in an interview that Obama's priorities should be as follows:

1. The economy
2. The economy
3. The economy[3]

Notice the trend?

Obama's greatest export to date to other countries: access to abortion.

And his insistence on hidden taxes on every American (cap and trade) was not helping America's confidence in the newly elected president.

President Obama began to see significant plunges in his approval numbers, particularly on policies. He did not rule a center-left nation, and that's why he was already feeling the pain and discomfort. In fact he didn't "rule" anything at all. We the American people had *lent* him the authority and the responsibility of administrating our nation's concerns for a brief period of time. He works for us.

In order to improve the situation in the near term, one of two things would have to change. President Obama would be forced either to move center right, or to be prepared to lose large numbers of allies in the Congress in 2010, and possibly the White House in 2012 (maybe even by a margin larger than his win in 2008).

The challenges he faced were grim ones. That is why I was praying for the president daily. It probably wouldn't have hurt for him to be returning to the practice of seeking God himself.

PESKY PUBLIC POLLS: CHENEY UP, OBAMA DOWN?

Seeing that polls give us little snapshots of what the appetite of the nation is like at any given moment, I found myself astounded by the moment we found ourselves in by September 2009: At that time, former vice president Cheney was on a two-month surge of popularity. President Barack Obama, on the other hand, was doing his best Wile E. Coyote impression, with no brakes on the rocket car, and was in the process of careening over the edge of the fifty-foot cliff.

So what had boosted the former vice president anywhere from 8 to 10 percent, while the president nose-dived 11 to 14 percent? I'm certain the layers to this answer are many.

The president had had a rough summer, and with his fall looking even more deficient in enthusiasm due to dropping employment numbers and even more depressing economics, things looked tough for the foreseeable future. People knew that unemployment during the previous administration had hovered in the 4 to 5 percent range for nearly the totality of two terms, and they longed for the days when they had jobs. Obama promised he'd personally never allow the unemployment rate to surpass 8 percent, but now with the rate rising to 9.7 percent, the president desperately wished he could somehow get back to that 8 percent number.

But I'm fairly certain that it was something more than that. The current administration didn't seem to understand that creating growth within the economy would help solve the most needs for the most people.

For instance, if someone has a job, he can choose whether or not he has health care. If someone has a job, she can decide to invest and save for the future, so that when tough times come, she's more prepared. Someone with a job can feed his family and give the ones he loves a better place to live. Having a job makes other parts of life get better for many, many people.

Vice President Cheney never forgot that helping the small business-person in America also helps both the individual's employees and his or her dependents, simultaneously. By cutting the tax burdens on small business (people the Obama administration had labeled rich and evil), you help provide livelihoods for a dozen families. By creating a smaller burden on small business, you create jobs, and jobs solve many other problems that Americans were now facing.

Yet again, I'm not truly convinced that this was the secret to why America was moving toward Cheney and away from Obama. Personally I think it came down to gravitas and the ability to look out for Americans.

President Obama seemed completely uninvolved in the actions of his attorney general, Eric Holder. Holder had become a bit problematic in that he seemed to be making wildly controversial decisions, and just running with them. One example is the public announcement that the Justice Department would go after former CIA officials who had interrogated terrorists captured on the battlefield. President Obama had even gone so far as to intimate that he cannot control the choice of cases

Holder decides to pursue. But even political novices aren't fooled by this kind of sophistry.

Security also seemed to just be a game to the current administration. That's fun to use politically (like pitting the Afghanistan conflict versus the Iraq theater during the campaign), until one day we woke up and realized that Afghanistan may be a bigger mess than Iraq was. Obama recklessly made speeches in radical regions of the globe, calling America a Muslim country and saying that Americans share the same values as Islam.

You see, Vice President Cheney, or Lord Vader, or however you refer to him, has a pretty opinionated view of terrorists, and not necessarily the kindest. You know, they did plan on flying an airliner into his office. The man was never confused over whether or not subjugation of women, honor killings, and female circumcision were "American values."

Furthermore, Vice President Cheney also strongly believes that the men and women who are asked to extract information from terrorists to save American lives should be given the legal protection they were granted by the Justice Department to begin with.

There was no reason to go open up new cases on the men and women who did their job, kept us safe, and had never so much as heard a thank-you from an administration that owed its very possibility to their success.

In short, Vice President Cheney believed there are such things as heroes, and he was just old-fashioned enough to step up and say so, even in public, and even contradicting the administration in power, if necessary. President Obama, on the other hand, asks Rahm Emanuel, David Axelrod, and Robert Gibbs if heroes exist, and goes with whatever two out of three say.

At the end of the day, serving "We the People" as president had turned out to be much harder than simply talking about being president. And doing so while trying to change the very fabric of what America fundamentally is had not been quite as easy as simply repeating the words "Hope and Change" while clicking one's ruby slippers together three times.

President Obama lives in a world that he desperately wishes existed. Vice President Cheney lives in the world that actually does. And as much as Cheney did not relish having to correct the current administration on policy, Americans were showing that they were grateful that he was taking the time to do so.

Well . . . 8 percent more of them over the months of July and August 2009, anyway.

MISLEADING THROUGH PLAIN SPEAK

The most accurate definition of one who is "forked tongued" is someone who says one thing but means another. Liberals have generally been forced to practice such a verbal dance because no one would elect them outright if they said what they intended.

In modern history when it comes to being forked tongued, President Barack Obama excels well beyond imagination. Like most of his foreign policy speeches on American national security, his commencement address to the cadets at West Point on May 23, 2010, proved my point. On that dreadful Saturday, President Obama spoke of his intent to shape a new "international order" as it pertained to a strategy to keep America secure. He implied in his speech that America should not claim the mantle or the right of self-protection or self-responsibility. He also referred to America's minimal role in "promoting democratic values around the world": "The international order we seek is one that can resolve the challenges of our times—countering violent extremism and insurgency; stopping the spread of nuclear weapons and securing nuclear materials, combatting a changing climate and sustaining global growth; helping countries feed themselves and care for their sick; preventing conflict and healing its wounds."[4]

In a disturbing trend, he chose to place absolute confidence in certain global institutions, such as the United Nations, but he has consistently believed less than he should about America, her fighting men and women, and the just causes they fight for.

Somehow international leaders who are not vested in America's well-being are to be believed as gospel, yet America is to be viewed with suspicion and contempt. It is an odd paradox that he maintains within himself. Keeping it to himself would be fine. Letting it spill into the mainstream is another matter entirely, and taking it to the West Point graduates is simply uncalled-for. Close scrutiny of Obama's involvement in world affairs demonstrates the exact opposite of what he had spoken of to the cadets.

Instead of countering violent terrorists, he has permitted them to commit attacks against U.S. citizens on American soil six times since his inauguration. The fact that the "underwear bomber" and the Times Square bomber got nothing more than smoke from their ignitions didn't mean that both attacks were not a severe danger to thousands of American lives.

Instead of stopping the spread of nuclear weapons, Obama has given every indication to Iran that he will do nothing to prevent them from gaining them. He's even gone so far as attempting to muzzle other nations who will suffer an even greater direct threat from a nuclear Iran—specifically, Israel, our closest ally in perhaps the world.

Instead of combating the false claims of the global warming propagandists who got caught by their own admissions in the lies, cover-ups, and inaccuracies they had promoted, Obama went before the American people and mocked any who did not hold the lies to be truth.

Instead of sustaining global growth, his policies of propping up companies that should've been allowed to correct on their own or fizzle out altogether have actually worsened the outlook for the average American, U.S. markets, and by extension, the global economy.

And instead of helping other nations become self-sufficient and responsible for their own laws, welfare, and futures, he's taken punitive action against allies such as Israel and Honduras, and played footsie with nations that we have in recent years considered dangerous. These include Syria, Yemen, Iran, and North Korea.

Later in his address to the West Point class of 2010, Obama said, "America has not succeeded by stepping outside the currents of international cooperation . . . but by steering those currents in the direction of liberty and justice."[5] The president was either woefully ignorant of America's contribution to history, or he was being purposefully misleading in such a statement. To be clear, America has primarily succeeded by stepping outside the currents of international cooperation, leading the charge to form new coalitions, and—when necessary—going it alone. We have often resolved to do so because of the moral demands placed upon us as the greatest nation on this planet.

From the American Revolution to the liberation of Afghanistan and Iraq, there were moments before us at every point that would tell us to "not get involved," to "let the rest of the world deal with it." There have been constant calls requesting us to let the world manage itself because America could not be the world's police force.

Yet when those same nations fell at the hands of tyranny, despotism, and economic and religious enslavement, it was to the United States that they turned.

Because President Obama is a nouveau libéral, he cannot simply come out and say what he wishes he could, for if he did, he would be impeached. But behind the mask of being moderate, reasonable, clean, and articulate (Biden's favorite qualities) lies a shadow of what he really believes. He is misguided at best, or a deceptive traitor at worst. Unfortunately, neither option brings us much consolation.

TIME FOR A BIT OF CLARITY

It is a reality of today—with changing technology, communication patterns, and the speed with which ideas can be translated—that vigilance in keeping freedom free will demand greater awareness, attention, and focus than in days gone by. Gone are the days when one party, one individual, one idea can be transmitted without evaluation. And while the trend was already moving in that direction, the election of Barack Obama has heightened it. It should not be surprising to us that the first president to ever be allowed to keep a BlackBerry or smartphone device of any kind is the same one who would eventually come to be known as the inspiration for the renewed birth of something called "the Tea Party."

The America that President Obama dreamed of creating had suddenly awakened an American populace who had no desire to see that brand of change come about.

Words matter, definitions mean things, and what we must—from this day forward—be prepared to realize is that sometimes they are used to trick and manipulate those they would later enslave. Tyranny, even when disguised in plain sight, even when practiced with a ruthless pragmatism that seems to lull many of the masses to sleep, must still be opposed.

CHAPTER EIGHT

Advancing the Non-American Agenda

The early days of any administration set the tone for what is to be expected in legislative fights in the days, weeks, months, and years to come. In Barack Obama's case the historic wave he rode to presidential victory was footnoted by the idea that change was something American voters desired, and he was determined to give it to them.

It's important that though his autobiographical books had sold hundreds of thousands of copies, very few Americans knew the degree to which President Obama had been influenced by non-American ideas, from his childhood in Hawaii and Indonesia to the outcasts he preferred to hang with in college.

He wrote openly that he preferred to spend time with the Communists; he liked their ideas. Because of his mixed racial heritage, he struggled with identity all of his life.

The America he saw, though it rendered him plenty of opportunity, wasn't always attractive to him. So the change that America needed, from his perspective, by necessity was different from what he had projected.

There was, however, also a much more cynical side to Barack Obama—the politician. For while his inner "lost boy soul" thought the ideals of socialized society were dreamworthy, the community activist inside him knew the force of hard-fisted machine politics—and also their pragmatism. Thus, before he was even an elected figure in Washington, D.C., merely campaigning for a U.S. Senate seat, he gave a speech on the Iraq theater of the war on terror. He didn't know anything at the time. He didn't have intelligence that the leaders of our nation did. And he hadn't seen the reports from intelligence agencies of more than thirty other countries that all came to the same conclusions.

But he wanted to stake out a position of being antiwar, and jumping into the fray on what he believed he could make a strong case for was the logical and most immediate way to make that noise.

In doing so he opposed the viewpoints of not only President Bush, but also former president Bill Clinton, U.S. senator Hillary Clinton, and the Democratic opponents of President Bush, vice president Al Gore and U.S. senator John Kerry. At the same time he strengthened his credibility on being something different to the progressive constituents he was already reaching, and he began to lay the mantra that would become his political battle cry as the face of "Hope and Change." It was not long, however, after he was in office, that though Americans had voted for change, they began to question if the change he had brought them was truly what they desired.

Early on he traveled to Egypt to speak at the University of Cairo. He delivered a speech within weeks of becoming president that equated the roots of freedom in the United States of America with the origins of Islam, a religious system that enslaves women and dehumanizes and kills opponents. He also not only roughed up our allies, but showed kindnesses to those with whom we had not been friendly for a very long time. Sometimes it even meant the loss of American sovereignty and property.

GIVE IT BACK, HUGO . . . YOU THIEF!

Should an attack on any group of Americans be considered an act of bad will? Should a hostile takeover of natural resources be considered a threat? Should a foreign power be given the right to unilaterally seize American assets with impunity?

Well, I suppose if you're Barack Obama, and the foreign power is Hugo Chavez, and the group of Americans is associated with natural resources—specifically oil and natural gas, the answer is obviously no!

Here are the specifics. As of June 24, 2010, at 5:28 p.m. EST, Hugo Chavez had initiated a hostile takeover of eleven oil rigs owned by the American company Helmerich & Payne. Helmerich & Payne have worked in Venezuela for more than fifty years.

Make no mistake; these rigs are not remotely mistakable as being the property of the government of Venezuela. But that made no difference to Chavez, and evidently not to the Obama administration, because as of the date of this writing, they've taken no action to force Venezuela to return the ownership.

Even more audaciously, Venezuela's "oil minister" went on national television, announcing the actions and claiming that Helmerich & Payne's rejection of a formal order from the Chavez government to resume drilling justified the takeover.

Leftists never call things what they actually are, either, so you have to understand their code to truly comprehend Chavez's aggression. He calls it "nationalizing," but in reality it is nothing short of felonies by theft. And when you consider the value and expense to drill each site with each rig, the cost of the theft is in the billions of dollars.

Now, would you like to know the truly secret irony of the entire matter? Helmerich & Payne had told Chavez to pound sand until he paid his bill. Estimates are that he is in arrears to the U.S. company to the tune of $100 million. Chavez's "oil minister" claims that Helmerich & Payne were violating the agreement by squabbling over "service prices." Back in the real world, Helmerich & Payne said, "We only want to be paid for the work already performed."[1] Come, now; people actually getting paid for the work they do? How dare they? The insolence! The capitalist pigs!

Evidently the announcement caught Helmerich & Payne by surprise, given that they were still in negotiations with Venezuelan puppets when the oil minister popped onto the television screens.

In response the weak-kneed imps over at the State Department marched out a pimply-faced junior spokesman who pronounced some very firm words about Venezuela needing to play nice or have more junior spokespersons from the State Department issuing other voice-crackling words. He also attempted to intimidate Chavez into submission, "This is the latest in such an instance where international investors, their investments are being nationalized by the government of Venezuela. It doesn't speak or bode well for the investment climate there."

Oh, that'll show 'em.

Problem is, in a world where deficit spending by governments is more common than oxygen, and in a universe where ownership of the value, material goods, and intellectual and physical property of your own work means nothing, this is only going to happen more often. Because truly, how different is it for Chavez to steal under the noses of the watching world billions of dollars' worth of equipment, property, and rights, and simultaneously refuse to pay what he'd already promised? Better yet, how different is either of those two concepts from the financial scale and model that President Obama has signed into law with the passing of his health care "reform"?

Government stealing is still theft. President Obama can afford to be laid-back about his buddy Chavez stealing from an oil company, because they are an oil company. Patriotism, loyalty to his own nation, responsibility to the citizens under his stewardship, and the moral principle of not taking what does not belong to you—all be damned.

Chavez has "nationalized" (i.e., stolen) dozens of companies within Venezuela's borders going on years now. But this is the first time he's performed a hostile takeover of a foreign-owned company or its properties.

In the neighborhood where I grew up, if Chris Greene or Daniel

Boone (two bullies who lived in my neighborhood) had tried to take my box of baseball cards, especially the one that had my 1972 mint Nolan Ryan card in it, they'd have had a fistfight on their hands that they wouldn't be forgetting about anytime soon.

But apparently when it comes to billions of dollars of U.S. property, resources, and revenue, Obama couldn't even be bothered to wake up from his midsummer nap. What's next? Giving California back to Mexico? Or maybe bringing the terrorists from Guantánamo to U.S. soil, since so many Americans believed that was a good idea . . .

THE TERRORISTS-FOR-JOBS PROGRAM

In November 2009, it appeared that officials in three states—Illinois, Montana, and Colorado—were salivating over the hope of landing a federal contract to house some of the remaining "Gitmo" detainees. The reason for such enthusiasm appears mostly to have been desperate economics. Amid reports the weekend of November 19 that President Obama's home state of Illinois was hoping to sell a prison facility to the federal government, the acting governor and senior senator from that state were calling it a "prize to be won." Here's how the Associated Press put it in their report:

> "In the midst of this recession, this is the good news we have been hoping for and waiting for and now we have to capitalize on it. The competition's on," Durbin told reporters Sunday. "It's a once-in-a-life-time opportunity." . . . The Democratic officials said the conversion could pump up to $1 billion into the local economy over four years and generate more than 3,000 jobs. That's potentially good economic news for the state that lost out on its bid to host the 2012 Summer Olympics.[2]

As the Democrats involved were spinning it at the time, the facility would not be of any threat to the state since they claim it would hold no more than 100 detainees.

I guess the logical questions were many. But three came to my mind:

1. Isn't a billion dollars of other people's money a little steep to create 3,000 jobs? (That's more than $300,000 per job created.)
2. In putting terrorists on the soil of your home state, don't you put your residents at greater risk?
3. Shouldn't a state's voters have the chance to weigh in on something of this magnitude?

If the creation of new jobs was truly a priority for this administration, as opposed to merely "saving" some, there were less expensive ways to go about doing it.

According to the MSA Report from the Illinois Coalition for Jobs in 2006—at the height of the small business tax relief passed by the previous administration—rural Illinois, without spending any federal dollars, saw more than 11,600 jobs created simply from the month of April 2006 to May 2006.[3]

I agreed at the time that job creation should be the single most important priority for the administration. But billions in spending given to political cronies in the president's home state seemed way too costly to be the right thing to do, especially when so much more could be done to create those jobs by merely extending the help that small businesses so desperately needed.

All right, so maybe letting other nations take American property and bringing terrorists to U.S. soil weren't such good ideas, but that didn't make him un-American, did it?

Well, is it "American" to take credit for something you have not done?

WHEN NOBEL WASN'T NOBLE

It was October 2009. President Obama had not yet been in office a full year, and the silliness that had catapulted him to the presidency was about to hit its most absurd high. Even though nominations for the award had been cut off eleven days after he took office, President Obama had been awarded the 2009 Nobel Peace Prize.

This presented the new president with a genuine dilemma. If he wished to be seen as a serious world leader, he should have declined the prize. Doing so would have been, in fact, the most honorable thing for him to do. A very simple expression of gratitude for being considered would've been appropriate. And a courageous footnote of honesty—by simply stating that because he had been in office for only twelve days at the time of the nomination, he had done nothing to deserve it, and that he would not feel at ease accepting the prize—would've been most refreshing.

Such a bold, courageous, and indeed masterful move would have underscored the humility he claimed to seek for America on the world stage, and it would have shown his critics that he was not as entirely one-dimensional as their mountains of evidence had begun to suggest. It was an opportunity to take a significant step toward a much more serious approach to leadership for which America could ill afford to wait a moment longer.

He did express an early and honest observation that he was not worthy of the prize. Partisan, even rancorous, Democrats had scoffed at the idea that he should be compared to Dr. King and FDR. Even NPR's own Juan Williams exclaimed the awarding of the prize to be utter foolishness. These observations, all from the political Left, were absolutely true.

In addition to making a statement about his nation's humility, and an even more significant one about his own, declining the prize would've done something else favorable for the president: wipe clean the slate of public perception that he was a man more concerned about his image than the substance of his office. In not declining, he missed that chance.

It was my sense at the time, and it has grown since, that the American people, many of whom supported President Obama, were growing weary with the "carnival dog barker" element of his administration. To be inundated with coverage of his self-indulgent Olympic-bid speech, as opposed to being focused on how our fighting men and women are losing their morale from lack of a clear battle plan, was, on balance, not something the American people wished to see. Because the same week he was nominated for the Nobel prize, the unseemly statistics on Afghanistan had been released. And while President Obama was about to receive a totally phony award claiming to promote peace, Americans were dying faster in combat than they had under Bush. Of the roughly eight hundred lives we've lost in Afghanistan during the first eight years of the Afghanistan war, fifty-seven of them had come in just the forty days leading up to Obama's Nobel nomination.

And corollary to this time frame, the military commanders on the ground in Afghanistan were requesting additional troops to accomplish their mission. While Obama weighed his response to the Nobel Committee, that request gathered dust on his desk.

The need for the president's attention went far beyond the crucial matter in Afghanistan. In just the previous week, Democrat senators had reinserted public funding for abortion into the health care bill. And on the House side of that debate, minority leader John Boehner was attempting to point out that since passage, the House version had seventy-five alterations to the bill. Many in the media and in the citizenry were questioning the legality of these "technical" changes.

In that same week, it had also been discovered that Kevin Jennings, President Obama's safe schools czar, has been linked to NAMBLA (a group that advocates sexual relationships between adult men and teen boys) and one of its iconic personalities, Harry Hay. Never has a more disgusting and revolting group of individuals existed, posing a threat to the welfare of America's children, yet President Obama put one of their supporters in direct contact with millions of schoolchildren.

President Obama had promised in his controversial commencement address at Notre Dame University earlier that spring that his administration would honor the "conscience rights" of health care workers, never forcing them to administer care or medicines that violated their own sense of right and wrong. But while the president was in between the jets from Copenhagen and Oslo, his administration was already breaking that promise. He refused to allow doctor's conscience protections to be included in the debate over health care reform. And in final passage of the reform measure, doctors were still unprotected in their efforts to practice medicine according to their conscience.

The president's supporters, particularly the vile ones who troll conservative Web sites, and the vindictive ones on social networks, had spent the last few days attempting to defend the "accomplishment" of President Obama in winning the Nobel Prize. In post after post, they repeated that he deserved it because he's taken a 180-degree turn from the Bush administration.

Yet informed people (even on the left) knew this was not the case either. American forces were still in the green zone in Iraq. We were still at war with terrorists. Gitmo still housed animals who could not be placed elsewhere, and that facility missed its latest rescheduled deadline to be closed.

The Nobel Committee specifically cited the president's speech to the university students in Cairo as one of the compelling factors that swayed their vote. Yet in that speech, President Obama claimed that the values of Islam and America were one and the same, and the last time I checked, we Americans do not take kindly to being told that we must subjugate our women, and we certainly do not find "honor" in murdering those in our family who embarrass us.

President Obama was getting used by the international elitists who had hatred in their hearts for an America that is both strong and good. He was getting played like a puppy given a treat for sitting still long enough.

In awarding Obama, the Nobel Committee permanently sealed its fate as an absurd laughingstock, but this time they'd made the president of the United States—and by extension our entire nation—the punch line.

If President Obama brings peace to the Middle East, or establishes free societies where neighbors in Afghanistan and Iraq live in harmonious community with one another, then he could legitimately win the award at a later date. But everyone on the planet knew that twelve days in, he had done nothing to earn it or the $1.4 million of prize money he would most likely give to ACORN.

No, if President Obama had wished to demonstrate greatness instead of pettiness, to display seriousness instead of taking an action that would cause him to be scoffed at, and to show his own commitment to making the world better, not merely talk about doing so, his solution would've been a simple one: he would've declined the prize.

Yet these examples paled in comparison to the most overt stab at the conscience of Americans, especially citizens of my city—New York. On these two issues he seemed completely tone-deaf too.

NEW YORK TO OBAMA: "NO, YOU WON'T!"

In November 2009, the Obama administration grossly underestimated the response of the American people in its decision—handed down by Attorney General Holder—to try accused 9/11 terrorists in criminal courts instead of military commissions. The American people were also not impressed that President Obama ducked responsibility for the decision to try them in New York by calling it a "prosecutorial" decision.

Americans saw the waste of money and resources that these trials would cause, and the harm they could generate by allowing them to proceed. Yet if all these things are true of Americans at large, the residents of New York City were even more affected.

Realizing that any criminal proceedings to move forward would take place on the same thirteen-by-two-mile island where the single biggest act of terrorism against our nation was ever committed, New Yorkers feel strongly that such enemy combatants, taken directly off the battlefields, should never be afforded Miranda and other rights associated with being citizens of the United States.

President Obama and Attorney General Holder had grossly mistaken the ferocity with which this case would bubble up and the inevitable media circus that would ensue. These trial proceedings—should they ever happen—will reopen the still-mending emotional, psychological, and physical wounds of 9/11. In deciding with such reckless abandon to make a political pay-off to the Far Left, and the radical Islamic sympathizers they ignorantly embolden, President Obama is ripping the stitches out of the hearts of those who have wondered if closure will ever come. When the attorney general promises courtroom cameras and complete transparency of the proceedings, he seems to ignore the possibility of radicals on camera shouting commands, jibes, and insults at those in the room as well as those sitting in caves across the globe.

The proceedings will create a bull's-eye again specifically on the most attractive target in America, and be used as an ongoing tool of recruitment. Without question, terrorists may have been upset over the treatment of their colleagues at Gitmo, but striking back at the base was a logistical impossibility. Not so with a city of endless train and subway tubes, elevator shafts, a metro area with a nuclear reactor only miles away, and an island that could be isolated and brought to a halt given the right combination of carnage and chaos.

The proceedings are an unnecessary move on the part of the administration to try these particular four terrorists at all. They have all confessed, and even bragged, on the record, of their exploits and parts played in the single worst moment in America's history. With on-the-record confessions, the seeking of the death penalty was ensured through military tribunal. What New Yorkers are now left with after the administration's move are mere words that Holder will "seek" the death penalty. And President Obama added his "assurance" that they would receive "the most exacting form of justice" possible. Yet if that was a foregone conclusion, why must he give assurances?

The insistence on having the proceedings in New York is a not-so-veiled attempt to continue to throw negative attention onto the previous administration. The real endgame of this matter is to reveal military and intelligence secrets for the public and our enemies to judge for themselves as to their legitimate use. The goal of Attorney General Holder in essence becomes the beginning of the reelection campaign for President

Barack Obama, and to create a way for George Bush to still be part of the discussion when the trials finally become a reality two to three years from now.

The proceedings also will cost enormous amounts of money in an era where we have none extra to spend. The process for trying each of these four terrorists would have to be reworked. Discovery, testimony, evidence that has all been worked and diligently put in place for dealing with enemy combatants taken in acts of war from the battlefield must now be sifted through a different standard. Depending on the political leanings of the judge assigned the case, it is even likely that many gaps will be left in the evidence path, and thus a jury will be instructed not to consider certain sections of otherwise admissible evidence.

I am hesitant to believe that even the Obama administration, with all of its harshest left leanings, would genuinely and truly want the mastermind and associates of 9/11 to ever walk free. But that possibility exists.

When O. J. Simpson was found not guilty, the jury saw the evidence of his blood mixed with Nicole Brown Simpson's on the scene, and in trails from one room to the next. And yet he walked. Should a similar outcome occur in this case, it would not shock me if we as taxpayers would be responsible for the cost of transporting confessed terrorists to their jihadist homelands, where they would go right back to work attempting to strike America again.

The average New Yorker understands all of this, as does the average American. They also clearly see that President Obama and his minions like Holder are willing to play games with national security in order to make a pandering play to their base.

This travesty will not sit well in New York elections in 2012, and unless President Obama decides to concede these basic concerns as legitimate by those who lost the most in our nation's worst nightmare, he'd best consider the electoral consequences.

New York City may be a town of liberals, but on the issue of national security, even we New Yorkers, in large numbers, are willing to set aside many other concerns to ensure the safety of our nation and our children.

One last parting note needs to be tucked in the back of the minds of the Obama administration, even if it doesn't give them much comfort: I wonder what a Democratic presidential primary candidate in 2012 by the name of Hillary Clinton will have to say to her fellow New Yorkers about such a wrong-headed and utterly foolish gesture. Stay the course, Mr. President, and we might just get an answer to that question.

And just as the possibility of New York City trials began to fade in the day-to-day consciousness of Americans, suddenly the president—not his attorney general—found a way to express himself on the most divisive issue of his first term.

9/11 WORDS ON OBAMA'S MOSQUE

It was something he certainly didn't have to do. But he did it anyway. President Obama stepped into the fray of the single most divisive issue pertaining to terrorism, healing of hurt, religious disagreement, civil liberties, political fracturing, racism, and national security all in one step.

How's that for bringing us all together?

Why a sitting president feels compelled to sit down to a formal Muslim dinner in the first place begs the issue of necessity. Although, to be fair, President Bush also held *Iftar* dinners in the State dining room. But in this case, Mr. Obama, why not send a nice little videotaped greeting, as you did to the Boy Scouts of America? I mean, it's not as if it was the 100th anniversary of anything, after all.

No, instead President Obama you felt compelled, not just to attend, but to host the little soiree and then make formal comments addressing the gathering. Something along the lines of:

> But let me be clear: as a citizen, and as president, I believe that Muslims have the same right to practice their religion as anyone else in this country. That includes the right to build a place of worship and a community center on private property in lower Manhattan, in accordance

with local laws and ordinances. This is America, and our commitment to religious freedom must be unshakeable. The principle that people of all faiths are welcome in this country, and will not be treated differently by their government, is essential to who we are. The writ of our Founders must endure.[4]

Question, Mr. President: Do you feel that *all* Muslims have a right to exercise their religion?

How about those around the world who buy into the exact same brand of radical Islam that the killers of 9/11 practiced? Do you feel that they have the right to practice *that* brand of Islam in the United States? How about on the hallowed space surrounding ground zero?

Even the "moderate" practitioners of that faith seem to be having some real trouble coming to clarity on not encouraging their fellow Islamists to be so insensitive. To date all of two prominent moderate Muslims have had the courage, and endured the death threats, to suggest the mosque be built somewhere else.

But you, Mr. President, we expected better of you, and Mr. Bloomberg, and Mr. Paterson, for that matter. We expected those of you who work for the American people to have some sort of understanding of propriety, decency, and honor. At the very least we did, and still do, expect you to demonstrate some modicum of competence: like pushing the Pause button until we know who is funding the mosque, and where the money comes from.

Also, a check into the known links between the front man for the effort and terrorist groups wouldn't hurt either.

The truth is, the mosque is in large measure being favored and given preferential treatment to other communities of faith. How else can you explain why a small Greek Orthodox church in the same neighborhood— which existed prior to 9/11—still doesn't have clearance or permission to reestablish its presence in lower Manhattan?

Americans aren't unreasonable, Mr. President. If we could be really sure, because some investigative body did its job thoroughly, that the kind of Islam being taught in this particular mosque wouldn't be the same kind of Islam that is taught in radical mosques all over the world, then we'd find it somewhat easier to be soothed by your forked-tongue comments.

The problem here is, no one's even claiming to have a desire to look into it.

In Islam there is a long-standing practice of building a mosque—a shrine to Allah's glory—upon conquered lands. I know that you and the rest of the "professional left" find it inconceivable that Muslims would dare to think that about America. But you've given them no reason to think otherwise.

You let your attorney general spit in the faces of the 9/11 families by attempting to bring the beasts currently housed at Gitmo back to my precious city to make some grand gesture. But the jihadists didn't see it that way. They laughed at you for your foolishness.

In fact, since you've been in office, you've repeatedly apologized to the Islamic world for America's wars (the ones that resulted in the liberation of fifty million Muslims,) you wholly redirected our space program to the unique purpose of making them feel good about how much Muslims have contributed to science, and on issue after issue you've sided with the views of the terrorists, even appointing several of the former defenders of the Gitmo detainees to your Department of Justice.

But regarding the mosque at ground zero, even though no one was asking you to, you stepped into the most painful issue related to the hallowed grounds of 9/11 to date. You chose sides. And now it's in your file. We will discuss it over the next two years.

TIME FOR A BIT OF CLARITY

If you had told me that prior to the election of President Obama there would be such rampant anti-American fever being spread by a sitting administration, I would've been hard-pressed to believe it. But I have not been the only one to observe it. Enough people over a long enough period of time—though far shorter than most could've imagined—said, "I don't like the direction this 'change' is taking us."

Voter's remorse was setting in. It roared in places where suddenly voters were actually reading the Constitution, the Declaration of Independence, and the Bill of Rights. They were learning about the history of the forefathers. HBO even produced a biographical miniseries on the life of John Adams.

And this awakening came not a moment too soon. For the most dangerous element in a debate of ideas is free thought. The second most dangerous is free speech. America, as of 2010, had not progressed to the Hugo Chavez–like conditions where his government took control of the media, but bills initiating that path had been pledged and promised by the Obama administration from the time he took office.

It was Mark Twain who once said, "Patriotism is supporting your country all of the time . . . and your government when they deserve it."

For President Obama, the country he works for and the government he is attempting to grow are at odds with one another. And that has been a *good* thing. The Tea Party movement has brought beneficial change to both political parties. In 2010 the major GOP sweep back into a balance of power wasn't one of just "go along to get along" but of genuine Constitutional principle.

But vigilance is necessary regardless of which power holds the reins, and the question remains as to how vigilant Americans will be in the future.

CHAPTER NINE

Deer-in-the-Headlights Foreign Policy

In June 2010 one of the most significant changes ever made in our nation's White House occurred. It was not the electing or changing of a party in power. The institution this impacted had survived many administrations.

Senior White House writer Helen Thomas resigned her job.

Most Americans were outraged at Helen Thomas's anti-Semitic statements, given to a rolling video camera with seemingly complete sobriety and coherence the week of June 6, 2010. But if Americans are honest, they would have to admit that the current administration's policies, positions, and preferences toward Israel come scarily close to agreement with the disgraced columnist for Hearst newspapers.

It is one thing for a journalist with ethnic origins from the Middle East to advocate over and over again across many administrations for the elimination of the Israeli state. It is another matter altogether for the first president in perhaps two generations to make the case that Israel should be left defenseless, so as to allow her enemies to eliminate her.

One is nothing more dangerous than rhetoric that only weak-minded people would absorb. The other is a dangerous position toward one of America's most important allies, in one of the most dangerous neighborhoods on the globe.

One makes a statement to a camera, knowing and understanding that what she is saying is being recorded, and will likely be revealed. The other has been running anti-Israeli subterfuge for the entire time in office. While intending to keep his bad behavior from coming to light, he did things such as making Israel's elected prime minister wait for hours unattended in a White House meeting room.

Helen Thomas has been cited spouting the view of terrorist groups, specifically Hezbollah, a group that has been and is still on America's terror watch list. Barack Obama has at every opportunity expressed dissatisfaction with Israel's domestic policy, even wishing to tell them where they may or may not build homes. He has done this while mostly ignoring terror threats from other noted terror states who have never relented from their promise to wipe Israel off the map.

Helen Thomas became rather infamous for regularly appearing to make assertions to support her "questions" that were more statement of opinion concluded with question marks. Barack Obama demands answers of Israel on moves they make to prevent groups from shipping dangerous weapons across open waters directly into Gaza and thus giving the terrorists ability to aim and fire on Israeli towns.

President Obama condemns the lack of international opposition to Israel's boarding of hostile vessels in waters off their shore. Helen Thomas condemned the right of Israel to shoot back at terrorists who were lobbing missiles into their territory from Lebanon (her nation of origin). Both have been largely silent on the disgusting video display of the animals attacking Israeli Defense Forces, brutalizing them with clubs, sections of pipe, and knives. Both have also been silent on the administration's position on a United Nations resolution that was passed late on a Friday afternoon (thus avoiding much media scrutiny), in which for the first time ever, the American administration sided against Israel and called for the tiny nation to eliminate its nuclear weapons. These weapons have kept the peace in the Middle East for several decades, never once having been fired.

President Obama has treated Prime Minister Netanyahu appallingly, multiple times. His efforts to handcuff the most significant ally we have in the region have caused the Israelis to realize that we might not be their best friend these days. His constant suspicious judgment of Israel has perhaps helped them understand that they may need to be more vigilant because they may have to fight alone.

Yes, in the immediate aftermath of the flotilla attacks, the administration put on a strict "we support Israel" face of support. But the president's heart was not in it then, and his distrust of Israel is notable even now.

Both believe it, but Helen Thomas said it, and President Barack Obama is attempting to legislate it.

It was right that Aunt Helen be put out to pasture from the media stage. But I'm of equal opinion that President Obama should have his agenda sent to the same place. Alienating allies is not the part of "Hope and Change" that America voted for.

Yet our treatment of Israel is only one example in which the Obama foreign policy team's decisiveness has been apparent.

Early in the administration one of our neighbors to the south, Honduras, had undergone an attempted coup of sorts by a president who was attempting to subvert the Honduran constitution. Instead of clamoring for the rights of the Honduran people and their constitutional law system, the president sided with the ousted criminal who had been trying a power grab. Hence, it was not surprising to see Hugo Chavez and Fidel Castro both speak publicly in support of Obama's position on the coup as well. Meanwhile, our more democratically inclined allies all sent verbal and in some cases institutional support for the people of Honduras.

TIME FOR A BIT OF CLARITY

Perhaps no better example of Obama's administration's unease in foreign policy has been exhibited than when the people of Iran, sensing that their most recent elections in 2009 had been stolen right out from underneath them, took to the streets.

A young girl from those street demonstrations became the face of the Iranian martyrs. She had dared to wear jeans instead of her Islamic dress, and she had chosen to wear a T-shirt instead of her head scarf that day. As she marched, the television cameras found her, and as the world watched, a shot rang out, piercing her chest. She bled to death within minutes.

Following that weekend's events, President Obama spoke out for the first time on the Iranian election controversy. He claimed that the footage had truly shaken him, that he had decided he could wait no more to speak, and that he was siding with the people of Iran. What horrible timing given that the street demonstrations were nearly two weeks old, and in fact were beginning to wane because of the brutal crackdown by Iran's republican guard. No American president should ever need two full weeks to decide whether he should stand for the freedom of individuals or for the controlling elite that sought to keep their people enslaved.

A simple lesson here is that freedom is always the correct answer. It's genuinely not any more complicated than that. When a controlling elite vies for control over the masses, freedom is always correct. President Obama simply isn't sure about this basic truth, and that is what causes him to question whether people's votes should count, whether we should condemn dictators, and whether or not the state should make decisions for the individual.

Unfortunately, this reality brings us to the harshest conundrum of American life: the place where freedom and security hit heads in an attempt to keep America both free and safe.

CHAPTER TEN

Why Obama Is Losing the Third Jihad

Throughout the summer of 2010, I traveled the country, speaking to groups of young people who were enrolled in the "Summit." For a number of years, Summit Ministries in Colorado Springs has offered these worldview boot camps for the most motivated, deep-thinking, and serious students in America.

Summit attendees are the cream of the crop. They know more about the intricacies of how their beliefs are tied to the rest of their lives than any group of people I've ever spoken to. But even these well-informed students were unable to answer a simple question for me when asked (most attendees of the first two 9-12 Project marches I keynoted in Washington, D.C., were equally unable to answer): "How many terror attacks occurred on American soil in the first twenty months of Barack Obama's presidency?"

Do you know the answer?

AMERICAN SOIL: TERROR TRAINING GROUNDS

As I pen these words, not more than sixty miles north of where I sit, a radical Islamist breeding ground is churning out hate, weapons training, and radical Wahhabi indoctrination. To date President Barack Obama's administration has done zero about it.

In fact there are *thirty* additional compounds like this one, spread throughout the nation in blue states like New York and red states like Virginia. And in each place the residents have been observed or overheard testing explosives, firing weapons, and engaging in the same type of activities.

Cutting to the chase, let it be plainly said: there are thirty-one (thirty in addition to the one I just described) bases of operation in which strongly questionable use of weapons training and militant jihadist principles are being taught here on U.S. soil. They are actively supplying clerics to serve in the prison chaplain systems across several states, and in many instances those who do are also actively recruiting new members for the future Islamic State of North America. Their stated goal on one of the chaplains' Web sites is for that state to be in existence by 2050. Since the compound, known as Islamberg, has more than two hundred residents, and since it took less than 10 percent of that to kill more than three thousand Americans on September 11, 2001, we would assume our nation's authorities would shut it down.

It would be of comfort for the administration to square with the American people that Islamberg is owned and operated by Sheikh Mubarik Ali Shah Gilani (aka "al Fuqra"), a known terrorist who currently funds and owns all thirty-one of the camps. The Pakistani terror leader remains out of the nation, but regularly provides instructions for those who operate these bases as to how to combat local law enforcement and to ensure that they never gain legal access to the compounds.

Federal authorities have yet to address these compounds with any serious attention.

It is not surprising, then, that the makers of the film *The Third Jihad* were so obsessed with letting Americans know what is happening behind our backs, down the street, and in the open rural areas we love. Enemies of America are seeking our destruction. It is an important film because the host of the documentary is an American Muslim, and one of the extremely few who has had the courage to speak out against the violent radical elements in his faith community in America.

The compounds, however, present only part of the challenge. The FBI unearthed a much larger issue, but little has yet been done to combat it.

Through a series of violent protests in Western Europe over things such as comic strips depicting Allah, journalists, media outlets, and eventually whole government systems began to make compromises. In each case free speech had limitations placed upon it.

In some cases, such as Great Britain, justice in Muslim neighborhoods is now according to Sharia law systems. In America, while hundreds of thousands of Muslims would argue that they have no desire to see Sharia law become the way of American society, nearly 25 percent of those same Muslims say they do believe that taking the life of the innocent in order to perform the will of Allah is allowable.[1] And honor killings are on a sharp increase among American Muslim families.[2]

Every American needs to understand the patient persistence with which the Islamic State of North America is being built. They also need to understand that the U.S. government is at this moment asleep to the problem that is festering here. And with President Obama's budgets cutting intelligence, defense, and national security spending, we've a very real reason to be concerned. This is especially true given the boldness with which others—such as the tyrannical terrorists in Iran, and the crazed and extremely dangerous nuclear power of North Korea—have dusted aside any concern about America while Obama is at the helm.

In my city in the spring of 2009, four men who had been recruited by elements of Sheikh Gilani's crew were caught attempting to place what they believed was a dangerous amount of C-4, intended to bring down an airliner and blow up a prominent Jewish landmark.

The worldwide domination by jihadists is real, and the president would do himself a favor by acknowledging the need to investigate those areas that are being used to plot our destruction.

Unfortunately, on six different occasions in the first twenty months of Obama's presidency, that jihadist mentality spilled out into real life. Beliefs became actions—actions that attempted to take tens of thousands of American lives. And the president's response to one of the most heartbreaking of the attacks painted a picture most Americans found discomforting.

FORT HOOD JIHAD

On November 5, 2009, Major Nidal Hasan opened fire on his fellow Army troops in a crowded medical building on Fort Hood, Texas. He killed twelve soldiers and one civilian, while shouting "Allah Akbar!"— Arabic for "God is great!" Finally, he was brought down.

In the hours following the shooting, President Obama demonstrated apathy to the greatest issue of our time. It was rather unbecoming behavior for a United States president, and the American people noticed.

Roughly two and a half hours after the shooting that took the lives of American service personnel, on American soil, President Obama was scheduled to deliver a speech to a Tribal Nations Conference being sponsored by the U.S. government. Once the president was told of the Fort Hood shooting, the White House team made the decision to go forward with the conference and have the president deliver his previously prepared remarks.

When the president took the stage, the news networks of the world zoomed in on the otherwise-obscure conference. He spent several minutes giving introductory remarks. He gave shout-outs to his "homies" in the crowd. He also apparently attributed a Congressional Medal of Honor to someone in the room—the only problem being that the man in question had never, in fact, received the Congressional Medal of Honor.

Eventually Obama turned his remarks to the violence of the afternoon and laid some less-than-Obama-esque sentiment on the gathered crowd and the watching networks.

But the rank and sophomoric way he began the speech was off-putting. Commentators for NBC even wrote in shock at the president's lack of protocol, sensitivity, or even awareness of the pain the nation was feeling at that moment.

But if all that were merely an innocent mistake by an increasingly wet-behind-the-ears rookie some nine months after taking office, what was to be revealed within the hour would be stomach churning. In his remarks President Obama called for everyone to remain calm and to not jump to conclusions about the cause, rationale, and motivation behind the shooting incident. Evidently what he meant was for Americans to disengage their minds from the truth.

Within the hour Stephen Hayes reported on a Fox News Special Report that sources inside the Obama administration's FBI leadership had confirmed that people involved in the investigation were told not to consider any possible connection between the shooting and terrorism.

Incredible . . . A man posts repeatedly on pro-terrorist Web sites for months, rants about being forced to serve in Iraq or Afghanistan despite his objections to the U.S. military being involved in those regions, and yells "Allah Akbar" before unloading his weapon—but his connections to terrorism were not to be "considered."

How could the FBI take such a posture? We real Americans would like to know.

Only a day previous the president demonstrated that he had genuine perception problems as it related to another concept: freedom. After German prime minister Angela Merckel's gracious visit, the Obama administration went out of their way to publicize the fact that the president would have no part in recognizing the anniversary of the fall of the Berlin Wall.

The Berlin Wall, of course, represents everything America stood in opposition to in World War II, and it was an American president and not a Soviet agent that ultimately caused it to fall. So why wouldn't President Obama wish to honor his *own* nation—and the cause of liberty universally—and recognize the date when the German people were united again after many years of forced separation?

Perhaps it boils down to the fact that this president does not make a distinction between a free state and an enslaved one. Perhaps he does not believe that life under Soviet cruelty was something we should pronounce judgment upon. Perhaps this is also the reason he sees little difference between the dictatorships in Iran, North Korea, Venezuela, Cuba, and countries that seek to live under self-determination, democracy, independence, and liberty.

At the University of Cairo speech in Egypt, which we've talked about previously, he equated the values of Islam and America as one and the same. He even calls us one of the largest Muslim nations on earth. (We are eightieth on that list.)

If President Obama cannot see the value of the freedoms we cherish, why not throw some "shout-outs" in light of national suffering?

TERRORISTS WIN IN 2011

It was the final week of November 2009 when President Barack Obama addressed the cadets at West Point and the American people in a prime-time television address. He did so with immense expectations. After all, how would he explain the fact that it took five months to claim that his strategy "was not wavering" from his own policy as it was expressed in March of that very year?

President Obama's lengthy speech on that night was a bag of confusion, poorly defined terms, badly defined objectives, and even less overall clarity. In one sentence he proclaimed that the effort in Afghanistan was the greatest threat to peace for the worldwide community, and in the next sentence he declared the deadline by which the military objectives must be completed. Message to the terrorists: Wait it out. Blend in. Pretend to be a non-terrorist until July 2011; then all will be well.

But since he couldn't come out and say that, and since he couldn't allow the man he put in charge to fail, the president had to find a middle ground. So, starting with a troop deployment by Christmas, General McChrystal was to begin to get the first few of the 30,000 troops the president decided to allow to go. That number—some 50,000 less than the general originally wanted—would be Obama's last chance to demonstrate that he takes the threat of terrorists seriously.

The president sounded defensive. Some of his verbiage harked back to his campaign stump speeches. He also looked awkward condemning the war in Iraq—explaining that he had always been opposed to it—while claiming the fight in Afghanistan was for something as simple as the harboring of Al-Qaeda.

Did he not know that Saddam Hussein also allowed Al-Qaeda operatives to operate openly in Iraq? If the policy was to go after those who harbored terrorists, and those who funded terrorists, didn't Saddam fit the bill? He even paid the families of suicide bombers in other nations $25,000 per suicide.

President Obama tried to speak about the war efforts in the two theaters as two separate wars, yet he betrayed blatant ignorance, or dishonest intention, in not admitting the very ties that bound them together. For example, even Osama bin Laden labeled the Iraq front as the primary fight in the war.

Obama had a tough job. He needed to explain how he would protect America, but he still had to pander to his antiwar base that has called for all our troops to be brought home.

In the end he adopted the Bush/Cheney strategy and the recommendations made from the Bush review completed in November 2008. He had asked the Bush administration to remain silent concerning the review's findings, but he eventually adopted the policies as his own in March 2009. Even after nine additional review sessions with his war council, he did not significantly alter the Bush/Cheney plan.

President Obama, in outlining his Afghanistan strategy on that November evening, had adopted President Bush's strategy for winning in Afghanistan. With one major difference: he instituted a stupid deadline. Now all our enemies had to do was wait us out for another eighteen months or so.

TIME FOR A BIT OF CLARITY

Obviously we cannot afford to be weak in terms of national security. We must continue to hone and prepare our defenses in readiness, no matter if the economy is good or bad.

For those who believe that defending America is the wrong track to take, it becomes more difficult to make the case when a new jihadist attack is unleashed on American soil, much less six—which was the answer to the question I asked the Summit attendees: three deadly shootings on military recruitment stations in the beginning of 2009, followed by the Fort Hood massacre, the incompetent bombing attempts by the Christmas Day "underwear bomber," and the summer of 2010's Times Square bomber.

The fact that the last two were so incompetent that they could not properly detonate their explosive devices should never be mistaken for proactive, thoughtful policy toward our national security. It is anything but.

Lastly, in our ongoing debate over southern border illegal immigration, it is important to note that according to sources I have in the U.S. Border Patrol, since 2003, upwards of 2,800 illegals who do not originate from Central or South America have been stopped on the border. Those 2,800 illegal aliens were from Saudi Arabia, Iran, Iraq, Pakistan, Afghanistan, and Egypt.

In the end, President Obama could easily remedy one of the biggest threats to our security with the identification and documentation of people who wish to come in. But it will take a commitment that runs even deeper than that. And we can help assure that commitment when we remind those who work for us in the halls of Congress and the White House that responsibility number one is the protection of America and her citizens.

CHAPTER ELEVEN

Obama's Belief That "America's Exceptionalism" Is a Myth

In the early days of the Obama administration, there seemed to be far too much willingness on his behalf to apologize for the United States to other world leaders, communities, and nations. I never fully understood this; in fact, I grappled with how it was even possible that someone who campaigned on the need to "humble" our own country ever got enough people to go along with it to elect him.

President Obama apologized for America in speeches to students in Cairo, to world bodies in the world's Islamic regions, and in interviews to Muslim media. Even when standing on European stages, the man apologized for our nation at every turn. It struck this American quite wrong. My suspicion was it did the same for many others.

It would also show that if he did not believe America was good enough to lead without apologizing for itself, he likely felt she was rather unexceptional as well. This would in time turn into one of the most grating realities for me to deal with personally. I don't like wondering if the man who runs my nation doubts her goodness, regardless of what he has to say about her greatness.

Yet that is the feeling in the pit of my gut from that first speech at the University of Cairo.

And as the terror attacks of 2009–2010 unfolded, I was reminded all over again.

CONTEMPT FOR THE POOR, CONTEMPT FOR THE NATION

"The investigation into the Christmas Day incident continues," Obama said on January 2, 2010, "and we're learning more about the suspect. We know that he traveled to Yemen, a country grappling with crushing poverty . . . It appears that he joined an affiliate of al-Qaeda, and that this group . . . trained him, equipped him with those explosives and directed him to attack that plane headed for America."[1]

President Obama, from his early days on the campaign trail forward, has always been quick to link terrorists (though he will not call them that) with poverty across the globe. The idea is dishonest, misleading, and purposefully misconstrues the point of the issue. It also gives Obama incredible cover, though it insults the very people to whom he made his many campaign promises.

In doing so, President Obama makes us weaker, causes us to look in the wrong places, and at the end of the day, this says a great deal about his own commitment to what is required to be his foremost concern: the safety of Americans. It is bad enough that the president is blind to the danger terrorists pose, but he should be ashamed about how he attempts to force us to view the world through his sorely out-of-focus, rose-colored spectacles.

The quote at the beginning of this section is from President Obama's

Saturday weekly radio address to the nation, nearly two weeks after the Christmas Day bomb scare. I'd like to congratulate President Obama for finally admitting that what was obvious to every American (with the exception of perhaps his own Homeland Security secretary) was finally evident to him as well: America was attacked by al-Qaeda on Christmas Day. The only reason it did not take the lives of a couple hundred Americans on that airplane is because the terrorist couldn't manage to ignite his undergarments.

But what if he had succeeded? Would President Obama still have taken more than a week to admit to the American people that the attempted attack was an al-Qaeda action?

It seems this president rarely grasps the obvious, except when he finally chooses to.

But the most appalling part of his speech on that Saturday was not his eventual embrace of what everyone already knew, but rather, his implication that poor people are the real enemies, a habit he has long practiced in public statements on the issue. Why do liberals insist upon declaring that terrorist enemies are poor? Why do they seem to connect poverty with terrorism (though they never call terrorism by its name)?

I've personally traveled to impoverished lands, perhaps even more than our president has, from Eastern European countries all the way to the African continent, Latin America, and Haiti, the poorest nation in our hemisphere and the third poorest on the planet. I've tasted, smelled, and felt the impoverished experience of our planet. And I have to tell you, I don't see the link to terrorism. I know the theory is that because (in Obama's mind) America is a rich, empirical, occupational power, we are the primary reason that the world suffers. Those who hold to that believe that the impoverished in remote places on earth develop anger for America because of their personal lack of material goods. Eventually, genius law professors like Obama will argue, poverty drives the poor to radicalization and jealous revenge.

The whole theory is hogwash. The vast majority of impoverished people I've met certainly would like greater material ease in life, more regular work, and a little bit of help from time to time. But I've learned another very real truth about them: from the Sudan to Haiti and beyond, they generally are more thankful for what they do have than anyone living in America.

The "poor" in America are still quite wealthy in comparison to the genuinely poorest of the poor in this world. Our poor live in a country that can and does give them every opportunity to overcome their situation.

By comparison ask any number of orphan children in sub-Saharan Africa what they want, and they never answer "the destruction of the United States." In fact, far more often than President Obama would ever admit, they have told me, they want to *go* to America.

I feel deeply offended that the president uses the poor as political tools and pawns to pass his agenda, then turns around and slanders their character by constantly linking them to the dregs of the world's evil. It is a well-known fact that the terrorists who carried out the 9/11 attacks had the means to go to flight school, live in America, and even spend money on strippers the night before the attack.

Does Yemen have poor people? Yes. Are they to blame for the attempted downing of Northwest Airlines Flight 253 on Christmas Day? No. Not because they are poor, anyway.

Someday it would be really nice if President Obama just once opened his eyes and saw terrorists for who they are: radical Islamic fundamentalists bent on the destruction of the United States.

TIME FOR A BIT OF CLARITY

So how can poor people from around the globe look upon America and see the goodness that President Obama sometimes fails to see himself? It's a question worth asking. Yes, the standard of living is higher in America—even for the poor—than anywhere else on earth. But I don't believe the answer is found in material issues alone. America is in large part, I believe, materially blessed because she has been spiritually blessed. God has prospered her for the good things she has done, and He has done so far longer than perhaps anyone thought He would have. No superpower has ever dared to use its might for greater good than America. No nation has brought more economic, spiritual, and legal freedoms to people on earth than America. No one has liberated people from more oppression than America. And no nation stands ready to help when others are in need the way America does.

President Obama does not see it, one would be forced to conclude, because he doesn't want to, but America is a shining light in a dark universe. When other nations suffer, their first thought beyond attempting to help themselves is usually, *If only America would help us.*

America defines its legal liberties as being from God Himself. I believe that this simple recognition of God's authority has ultimately been an umbrella of blessing to those of us fortunate enough to call ourselves American.

May this ever be!

PART THREE

Erosion of Rights

CHAPTER TWELVE

Eroding Absolute Truth

If the ruthless pragmatism of Barack Obama is his greatest weapon, then the ammo is his convenient flexibility on such things as absolute rights, absolute values, and above all, absolute truth. See, if those rights, values, and truths are unchangeable, then as a man who values the ability to pivot and pump-fake, he cannot adroitly implement an openly anti-American agenda, one that encourages the implosion of free markets, wishes for larger amounts of government intervention, and seeks to punish those who disagree.

Since he can't openly pursue that agenda, instead he would have to cause things to appear as one thing, but focus on something else entirely. And always running in the background is the goal for changing reality altogether, like a computer that runs two operating systems simultaneously. This very methodology was employed from the beginning.

In the days of President Obama's campaign, he attempted to create government dependency by arguing for the concept of "caring for one's brother." And though there are many different ways to "care for one's brother," the only narrative he allowed to be expressed from those who hogged the spotlight and stage was through government intervention.

Sometimes when it allowed him to score a point, Mr. Obama would be content to allow his fellow partisans to state outright lies to the American people as part of the larger strategy of overall deception of his long-term agenda. The president was so insulated that—regardless of his ability to convince—his belief that he knows better than the American people allowed such hubris that he missed it altogether when the people began fighting back.

If the erosion of rights has a first victim, her name is Truth, and her defeat was necessary for the Obama agenda to become what he believed it could—the transformation of New America.

THE MOST IMPORTANT POLITICAL TRUTH OF ALL TIME

If you wish to see an enjoyable evening with friends become quite animated, then overly hostile, and end in exacting bitterness, ask those in attendance to choose between the following:

As an individual citizen, is it more American to believe that you have a personal responsibility to be accountable for your actions, and those of your family? Or is it more American to believe that you should wait for the giant collective to take care of you?

This wasn't always a controversial concept, until liberals decided that power is more highly coveted than freedom. Once they did, they started systematically enslaving people to the collective. Take the president, for example.

President Barack Obama's failures to stop smoking were revealed publicly in his first two official physicals once in office.[1] His refusal to stop smoking, and his need, according to the White House physician's official diagnosis, to "moderate his alcohol consumption" are red flags, health-wise. In fact, aggressive or non-moderate alcohol intake and cigarette smoking contribute to many poor health factors that do not show up immediately. Yet everything from heart disease to various cancers can be accelerated due to these behaviors.

But in President Obama's world, personal responsibility seems to mean barely anything, and the nation that voted for him reviles it.

On my nationwide morning show on March 2, 2010, I asked this very question, and the responses floored me. Geographically speaking, it made no difference. From east, west, north, and south, listeners declared repeatedly—and attempted to justify their belief—that the collective has more responsibility for the individual's happiness than the individual does.

And friends, if this is what the nation believes, we've lost America.

The reason our founders were so attentive to individual rights, and focused so hard to embed them into the bedrock of our founding documents, was because they understood that to be at the mercy of the collective was in fact to be at the mercy of a powerful few—not the generous masses.

President Obama may not wish to curb his habits as it relates to his health. But if he wants to engage in such risky behavior, he should not expect to have other people pay for his cancer surgery, his diseased liver, or the eventual recovery from a stroke or heart attack, should the unthinkable occur. Of course, he will be guaranteed all of that and more through the taxpayer employment benefit we bestow on him for his service to us in office.

He will argue again and again that it should be the requirement of the neighbor who eats fresh vegetables to pay for the costly therapy of the guy who lunches daily on Big Macs.

Liberals claim the collective owes the individual, while elected liberals who hold office make such arguments to attain greater power as the masses become enslaved to entitlement, falsely thinking they're getting what is owed them.

In reality, God stated that we are to provide for and protect our own families. He has warned that lazy men should not receive the fruits of other men's labor. And He made it clear that if a man does not work, he should not eat. (Meaning that intentional slothfulness is not to be rewarded if society is to function properly.)

The irony of all this is also not lost on me.

Individuals who know in their hearts that they will only rise or fall by the results of their own efforts, also tend to be the people who are the most generous with those who do fall on hard times. They give billions of dollars each year to ease hunger and suffering in other lands, and still take dinner to a next-door neighbor who just lost his job.

Those who sit waiting for the collective to care for them do so at the expense of the survival of free society.

But if you're President Obama, or any one of his millions of supporters, what do you have to lose? Hey, if something bad does happen . . . he doesn't have to pay for it!

LYING TO CANNIBALIZE, LETTING IT HAPPEN

"Nancy Pelosi has more integrity in her pinky than Dick Cheney and Karl Rove have in their whole bodies combined."

Some congressional idiot made that claim to a bevy of media cameras gathered for a press conference designed to help the flailing Speaker of the House try to save face, midway through 2009.

The issue was a bit of a scandal because Ms. Pelosi had just reiterated multiple times that she had never been briefed on interrogation techniques being used on the battlefield and in American detention facilities holding terrorist detainees. Because of Ms. Pelosi's longstanding opposition to nearly the entirety of the War on Terror, for her to claim she had not been briefed gave her an out on taking any responsibility for the interrogation methods. Shortly following, her words were proven inaccurate when Leon Panetta, President Obama's director of the Central Intelligence Agency, released a memo stating in no uncertain terms that Ms. Pelosi was lying to Congress, the administration, the media, and to the American people. Panetta also made clear that the CIA had truthfully and fully briefed the Speaker as to the techniques used, that she was in attendance, had acknowledged the techniques, and had no problem with them at the time.

Thus—the history books may say—began the downfall of Nancy Pelosi, former Speaker of the House.

It's one thing for her to try to pretend that the only voices contradicting her abhorrent memory of certain events were from the GOP. But when the new face of the Democratic establishment labeled her a liar, she had more trouble on her hands than anyone in her party wanted at that stage of the historic Obama presidency.

Obama was content to let her twist in the wind because his agenda has nothing to do with protecting her name and legacy as Speaker. But Pelosi's actions did cause thoughtful observers to wonder why she chose the path she did. Pelosi hadn't just told untruths. She had accused the CIA of conspiracy—against only her. That the CIA would feel the need to go to such lengths would be sort of like trying to kill cockroaches with bazookas. It would get the job done, but a little excessively.

For that very reason, Pelosi's version(s) of events was implausible from the beginning. Once she backed herself into the corner and pointed the finger at our intelligence community, she forced Panetta to release the actual record of what happened, and thus she had sealed her reputation forever. Nancy Pelosi is a liar, so labeled by her own party, the administration she serves, the party that opposes her, and the media. And there's little else that all those groups ever would agree on.

So why did she do it? It's simple. Liberals believe that nothing that comes out of their own mouths can ever be classified as a lie because in their reality, there are no objective facts or substance, only shades of interpretation. The fact that Pelosi was at the briefing didn't mean she was physically there, or if it did and she felt emotionally disconnected from what was being discussed, or if her mind wandered, then she wasn't really there, was she?

The fact that the intelligence officials at the briefing showed a complete and thorough demonstration of what waterboarding is, made mention of its use, and declared their intention to use it under limited circumstances in the days to come didn't mean she knew anything about it . . . right?

Liberals don't know things—like the definition of "is"—objectively, but rather, only what they are told, what they choose to believe, and what they intended for things to mean. Actual substance, definitions of words, and indisputable facts are all things that can be explained away or understood to be something else entirely, anything other than what they actually are.

It actually stems from a very sad reality for them all, a lack of belief in absolute truth. If nothing can be seen, understood, or intended to be absolutely true—then nothing is true, everything is subjective, and the only person who gets to decide is the person speaking at the moment.

This is how liberals operate.

Adultery is not engaging in oral sex with someone who is not your spouse. Marriage is not the sanctified union of a man and woman. Tax cuts can be given to people who do not pay taxes. Waterboarding is torture, though it leaves no scars or permanent damage. Nationalizing the banks, car companies, and mortgage industries is not socialism. Increasing gun control is not taking away second amendment rights of citizens. Closing Gitmo doesn't mean shutting it down. Abortion is not taking the life of an innocent human being. And for this president especially, letting live newborns starve to death in soiled hospital utility closets is just allowing a woman the right to choose.

Nancy rose through the ranks with the president who does this the best. He even wagged his finger at the American people, looked them straight in the eye, and told whoppers. But when liberals do it, it's not lying.

The people of this nation deserve better.

Nancy had a perfectly acceptable way out of the mess: tell people that following 9/11, she felt that waterboarding was an acceptable thing to do to save the lives of Americans at risk, but that now she has changed her thinking on the issue. In essence that is exactly what happened. And if she had, she wouldn't have had to go into hiding from what became a relentless pursuit for the facts. Mr. Panetta had already established more than enough headaches for her on that front. And for what it's worth, I also don't think that plugging her ears, clicking her heels, and screaming, "Bush is the devil" will bring her much comfort either. And for a president who was enduring sluggish approval at the time, letting Speaker Pelosi bite the turf for a while was helpful, because it kept the voters distracted from the quiet operation of his hidden agenda.

As the freshman season of President Barack Obama rolled into calendar year two, his staff and administration were all in danger of making the worst political mistake of their lives. They seemed unable or unwilling to recognize the damage this mistake would cause. And this reality might be America's brightest reason for genuine hope and change.

In August 2009, the actual "rulers" in this nation had a chance to speak. In high school gyms, in church basements, and in community college auditoriums, the first real chance for accountability was measured against the most tone-deaf administration of my lifetime. Retirees, stay-at-home moms, young professionals, and even a working bloke or two had shown up at the town hall meetings to hear from their representatives, and then to respond to the ideas put forth.

The report card for the administration in these town halls reflected the concurrent plummet in Barack Obama's approval rating on his signature issue—the universal federalized takeover of the health care system in America. By then only 36 percent of Americans trusted the president on the issue, while 53 percent did not.

Everyone on the president's team seemed taken by surprise at the angry response, primarily because of the biggest mistake an elected official can make: they believed their own press. When an administration has had as free a hand in turning the press corps into an echo chamber for its own policies as this one, they run the risk of believing what that press corps writes, reports, and editorializes upon. Instead of being the objective questioners they should in probing the depths of policies, intentions, and use of the federal agenda, the press becomes more or less a public relations extension of the executive branch. And the administration fell into believing what had been written, and honestly thinking their plan to take over the health care system of the nation was a mandate.

Yet in town hall after town hall, they were not able to control what "We the People" actually believed. The administration, the elected members of Congress, and most important, the president evidently needed reminding of who they work for. They needed help remembering what their obligations are. And they needed to be mindful that if they did not do what the board of directors believe to be best, we could toss them out with the next election like yesterday's kitchen scraps and start over again.

I personally was deeply moved and encouraged by the genuine efforts of citizens just like you and me attending town halls in August 2009. I became even more grateful, deeply so, that Americans had not become comrades of malaise, but rather, still had core convictions that could be offended, and were, in fact, angry.

This White House said, "Let me be clear," but followed those words with vague, noncommittal language, because they refuse to tell us the truth. They said in prime-time press conferences that the "public option" won't change current insurance coverage. But they told the thugs and buffoons of SEIU and ACORN that the public option will lead the way to a "single-payer" system. The administration said it will have the most transparent dialogue in the history of the nation. But they sent the SEIU guerillas and the ACORN equivalent of the Sopranos to town hall meetings in order to muscle out legitimate citizen dissent.

The administration said it would not keep or form a database of the snitches they begged to report on their neighbors who disagree with the health care plans. But under the federal laws governing all communication with the executive branch, they were required to keep the names, e-mail addresses, and correspondence sent to them on the matter.

The president campaigned on the idea of bringing people together from all sides to solve the problems facing us. But when he did not think a camera was rolling, he stated that he didn't wish for people opposing his view to do any talking.

President Obama deceived the American people. "We the People" gave him the benefit of the doubt, but in his first eight months, his actions betrayed his true intent, and we trusted him no more. Americans by an overwhelming majority had listened to the ideas behind the health care system reform and rejected it. They did so while admitting they would like to see reform, but not the sort that the president proposed.

Should the administration not choose to recognize the truth in this scenario, "We the People" reserved the right to send them to the unemployment line, and on November 2, 2010, we made that clear to them.

TIME FOR A BIT OF CLARITY

Whether it was the outright denial of the most important truth for a society to embrace (that a man is fundamentally responsible for himself and his family), or allowing colleagues to fall so his agenda could continue to move forward, or refusing to see the truth when those opposing him shouted it in town hall meetings, the erosion of truth was a necessary and vital part of the Obama strategy.

Unfortunately, this type of disconnect from reality, this lie of all lies—that the elected are not accountable to the electorate—has plagued forgetful politicians of all parties. What made it different with President Obama was that he was so brash about being insensitive to the truth. Most Americans couldn't believe anyone would be so bold with willful deception. And the reality was, he almost got away with it. Had the economy been even slightly better, the day-to-day pressure of endurance would not have been weighing on voters so strongly in the 2010 election cycle.

And for what it's worth, should the president choose to do an about-face on some of the most extreme positions and become more moderate, the way President Clinton did in his first term, the public might be lulled back into a quasi-hibernation of being financially fat and happy, and it might just lead to a successful reelection bid.

Personally, I think President Obama is a tiger of a completely different stripe than President Clinton. Clinton was ruthlessly pragmatic about staying in power, while Obama is ruthlessly pragmatic about transforming Western culture. He wants it truly more socialized, more Marxist, statist, and government-centric.

He wants America to be different from what she is, and unlike President Clinton, in order to make that happen, President Obama seems willing to scar an historic presidency with dismal public approval and incredible hostility from the voters.

CHAPTER
THIRTEEN

Re-creating Culture with Rainbows and Fairies

Complete re-creation of the culture through ruthless pragmatism was not limited to mere philosophical moorings or economic philosophies. As with Marxism, there were social, moral, and religious components to the worldview that had taken up residency in the Obama White House. And as with Marxism, there would be natural fallout on all of society because of it.

Marx believed in controlling the avenues of education available to the student, and the American Left, but especially the Far Left (of which President Obama is a member) have often believed that changing the schools, the curriculum, and the purpose and outcomes of education would be an effective strategy to changing America's long-term value structure. They are entirely correct, which is why President Obama's appointments to the issue of education were such disasters.

While the president was in Cairo, preaching Islamist propaganda to Muslim students in the early days of his presidency, his administration was carrying out an even more sinister agenda. He quietly nominated a man to be our "Safe Schools Czar" who teaches students to hate parents. While President Obama seemingly praised the earliest traces of recognition of Sharia law on U.S. soil (women being forced into wearing hajibs even in America), he stealthily put forward a nominee who refused to report a sexual relationship where a man was molesting a school-age boy, even though the law required him to submit a report of it.

In a documented case that Jennings now admits to, he once counseled a young boy who had been molested by an older male teacher. The confused student naturally turned to an adult figure for explanations, support, and direction. But when this issue came to Jennings's attention, even though the law required his notification of the parents, the school district, and the local law enforcement authorities, he now admits he notified no one. He expressed no regrets for his actions then, and has never indicated that if a similar situation were to materialize, he would follow any different path.

To wit, Obama sought to distract with his own, "Once, Twice, Three times a Muslim" act in Cairo, all the while praying that no one would notice that a protector of a child sodomist was being given access to children in our public schools.

Kevin Jennings was not just your normal activist nominee. He was a firm advocate of mandated affirmation of approval of homosexual actions by schoolchildren, and to this end, his involvement with the Gay, Lesbian, and Straight Education Network's (GLSEN) "Day of Silence" had moved them to go beyond that to demand "queer proms" in the local public schools, and to lobby for legislation in each state to change the definition of marriage to make it mean something it has never meant.

With Jennings's support, the GLSEN chapter in Connecticut had begun pushing not just for "tolerance" or "acceptance" in the public schools of those who chose to engage in homosexuality, but they had actually created an "activity" for the school systems that pushed "positive levels of attitude," such as mandated "admiration" and "nurturance."

In his past, Jennings has left quite a swath of destructive choices, as well. He authored the foreword for the book titled *Queering Elementary*, which argued for the teaching of sexual "identity" (what you could easily call "indoctrination," "initiation," or "brainwashing") to the children in elementary school. The book is so disturbing that it "praises teaching masturbation to a seven-year-old girl."[1]

Jennings also had a reckless past of undermining parental rights, even usurping them altogether on his own whim.

Admittedly, during those early days, President Obama had a rather ugly run of horrible nominees: finance people who cheated on taxes, Cabinet members who slandered our servicemen and -women serving at Gitmo without checking facts (or admitting their mistake later), and a Supreme Court nominee who evidently had been saying for more than a decade that Latina women are morally superior to white males. But the nomination of Kevin Jennings as assistant deputy secretary to head the Office of Safe and Drug-Free Schools broke new territory, one that endangered the health, happiness, and welfare of your child, and every other child in the public education system.

The role for which Jennings was nominated has a nearly accountability-free hand to institute a policy of normalization of sexual deviancy in the schools. He has the ability to operate with no real checks or balances, and with aggressive intent to push the envelope. His nomination in the shadow of night empowered those who seek to change the values, thoughts, and principles we as parents are attempting to instill in our children.

This early attempt to push through an advocate of sexual deviancy should've been swatted away, with fervor, for the safety of our children. In doing so, not only would they have been protected, but the president would've been able to see that we still had the vigilance to measure his actions and hold him accountable.

After all, he works for us, not the other way around.

TIME FOR A BIT OF CLARITY

Unfortunately, Mr. Jennings was not the first—or the last—controversial nominee put into high office. Others who sought to push the envelope— and to use our children's minds, classrooms, and lives—have made their way to power.

Yet it is important to remember one key element in this process: "We the People" made this possible. In not vetting the man who would be our president more carefully, we failed ourselves. In not understanding, investigating, or evaluating what his past political allegiances had been, we did not prepare—and we *were* not prepared—for the nominations, ideas, and policies he put forth.

In the 2010 elections, the nation began reclaiming that vote.

It's significant that more absentee ballots and more early voting ballots had been requested and returned at one week prior to the election than in the race of 2008. That is unusual because it was a midterm election; there was no presidential race involved. Yet the nation was—in as quick a way as possible—sending the message that the ruthless pragmatism that sought total national transformation was not the desire of the people.

Much is being speculated on what will occur in 2012. It will depend on what the people of these United States allow President Obama to do in his second half of his term. Yet one thing is sure; somewhere between 2008 and 2010, the people decided they would take back control of the direction that Washington sought to impose. And from where I sit, in America's grand scope of history, those moments have always been our best ones. Self-correction is one of the beautiful mechanisms our founding fathers left us with in the Constitution. Yet they did much more than that, when you think of it. In reality, they desired us to invoke it to protect the Republic whenever danger raised its head—from within or without.

CHAPTER FOURTEEN

Re-creating the Definition of *Person*

To adequately understand the erosion of our rights—and, more important, to track the ways President Obama and his administration wish to erode them—one need look no further than the very definition of what makes up a human being.

As a legislator for the State of Illinois, as a United States senator, and eventually as a president, Barack Obama went to extreme limits to keep the status of persons an undefined issue. He did so in part to satisfy differing constituencies of his key progressive left base. Yet in doing so President Obama threatens the validity of all constitutional protections.

One could learn a good deal about who candidate Obama was when he was campaigning for the United States Senate. In fear of appearing a bit too soft on the issue closest to the heart of one his deepest-pocketed supporters—Planned Parenthood—President Obama enlisted the bride of his youth. And in a letter that went to voters across the state, Michelle Obama assured the women of Illinois that her husband's commitment to supplying women's unfettered access to abortion need not be questioned.

Of course, only months before, as a state legislator, Obama had given proof of his own. He voted not once but on three different occasions for the blockage of a new piece of legislation that was designed to allow children to live, even if in the process of being born, they had originally been slated for abortion. In other words, if a doctor made a mistake while performing an abortion, and the baby was unintentionally born alive, this legislation would have required that the baby receive medical care.

The attempt to thwart the passage of the state version of the "Born Alive Infant Protection Act" was not widely highlighted in President Obama's candidacy for the White House, yet it should have been, for it betrayed his own belief that these babies are not people. That a life sometimes was not "worthy to be lived."

And as the slippery slope goes, if you believe that about one group of people, what's to keep you from eventually classifying additional groups the same way?

DIRTY BEGINNINGS AND DEADLY EXPORTS

Not yet in office a full seven days, President Obama put his signature to an executive order that reinstated taxpayer-funded abortions of hundreds of children across the globe. His executive order reversed the "Mexico City Policy," which prohibited funding to international family planning groups that provide abortions. It essentially barred recipients of U.S. foreign aid from promoting abortion as a method of family planning.

You were allowed no say in this. There was no "opt-out" box to check. Our tax money was now inextricably linked to the systematic deaths of these children. Their cries were not heard, and no leftist, progressive political group rallied in Washington to end the violence against them. Celebrations in feminist and pro-abortion offices resounded across America. How perverted is it to celebrate the ability to pay for the death of a child?

In other countries, many of them third world, a family's child is one of the few sources of joy a home can know. By reissuing this policy, Barack Obama had sentenced more Latin and black children to death than if he had simply ordered an invasion of Mexico or Somalia.

For all of his campaign rhetoric promoting the ideas of Hope and Change, such callous and calculated policies flew directly in the face of his claims to care for women, his desire for justice and fairness, and his professed faith in God.

As a pundit, I had repeatedly expressed my well wishes and desires for our president to succeed during his days in office. I was vested in my president succeeding for the good of my country. Thus, to extend fairness and even goodwill to the new commander in chief, I resisted the inclination to speculate on likelihoods, and pledged to wait on the formation of policies before leveling criticisms.

I had been prepared to give him longer than four days.

But in just his first week in office, he demonstrated his hardened ambivalence to those who love children as Christ instructed them to.

I did not wish his term in office to be plagued by racial dishonesty. His inaugural achievement that week was historic. His action on abortion just a few days later was both sickening and disheartening.

AN HONEST COMPARISON

March 1, 2009, saw a bold move as the president broke a sacred barrier that the American voter had every right to be deeply concerned about.

He exercised for the first time a policy decision that shared a trait held in common with Adolf Hitler. The headline was leaked late in the Friday afternoon news cycle so that as few people as possible would pay attention, but here's the crux of what turned out to be a very real problem: President Obama was moving policy on public health into the direction of doctors being forced to act against their conscience. He wanted them performing abortions whether they believed it to be an immoral thing or not. And while the comparisons to Hitler are made either on eugenist or racist grounds, you cannot escape the impact.

In the 1930s and '40s, as Hitler wished to use his captive "lesser-humans" for "experiments" in his final solution, he, too, forced doctors to do things they did not wish to do, from injecting living humans with untested chemicals to see the effect, to trying differing grades of poisonous gases in what eventually became the death chambers. These doctors who were supposed to help save lives were suddenly forced to use their medical knowledge to end them.

In today's scenario Obama wanted doctors to exterminate "lesser humans" for the purpose of immediate solutions to his social experiment. He called for an end to exemptions doctors had always had if their conscience prevented them from performing abortions. It was a purely pragmatic, political move to pay off the campaign favors of those special-interest groups that helped him get elected, in this case, the abortion industry.

This policy shift that Obama had attempted to slide under the radar screen was grossly immoral, and doctors were right to disobey it and run a medical mutiny against the administration when it became law. This stroke of the policy pen moved the administration into its first conflict with the First Amendment right of religious belief and expression.

President Obama had taken a demonstrable step in the shoes of Adolf Hitler.

OBAMACARE'S SHOP OF HORRORS

President Barack Obama took a unique and quite macabre strategy into the August recess of 2009. In speech after speech on the "need" for the federalizing control of a national health care system, President Obama had taken to insulting and demonizing the wrong people—physicians. I believe in doing so he was demonstrating the degree of deception to which he is willing to stoop, all for the cause of the fundamental transformation of the American health care system.

Roughly one month previous, President Obama stated in a press conference from the White House:

> "So if you come in, and you've got a bad sore throat, or your child has
> a bad sore throat, or has repeated sore throats. The doctor may look
> at the reimbursement system, and say to himself, 'You know what, I
> make a heck of a lot more money if I take this kid's tonsils out.' Now
> that may be the right thing to do but I'd rather have that doctor mak-
> ing those decisions, just based on whether you really need your kids
> tonsils out, or whether it might just make more sense just to huh . . .
> change . . . huh . . . maybe they have allergies, maybe they have some-
> thing else that would make a difference."[1]

In one swipe he slandered thousands of the very best pediatricians and ENTs (ears, nose, and throat specialists) across the board. He strongly implied that those who practice medicine are driven by greed, and not the welfare of their patients. Yet let me ask you this: how many children's doctors has your family had? In many cases one doctor has been the family pediatrician for two to three generations of children, and extended family, and friends of that family. In all honesty do you think that would be the case if they were treating kids like clunkers that can be cashed in for parts?

Roughly two weeks previous, President Obama said at a town hall meeting:

> "Let's take the example of something like diabetes, one of uh . . . a
> disease that's sky-rocketing, partly because of huh . . . obesity. Partly
> because it is not treated . . . huh . . . as effectively . . . as it could be. Right
> now if we paid a family . . . If a family care physician, works with his or
> her patient, to help them lose weight, modify diet, monitors whether
> they are taking their medication in a timely fashion. They might get
> reimbursed a pittance. But if that same diabetic ends up getting their
> foot amputated, that's $30,000, $40,000, $50,000, immediately the sur-
> geon is reimbursed."[2]

There he was again with the profit motive. Only this time he was actually making the argument that the doctor would be so malevolent as to not work with his diabetic patients to improve their condition, just to cash in. I cannot say this strongly enough: his willingness to view doctors with such contempt and disrespect sickened me, as it did nearly every medical practitioner in the nation. As best I can tell, there is no other industry that swears to the ideals of such a lofty vision as is found in the Hippocratic Oath. Yet their allegiance to such an oath is lost on the man who placed his hand on a Bible and took his own oath to uphold our freedoms and responsibilities as outlined in the Constitution.

On the issue of payment for foot amputation, he was also factually wrong. And given the extreme amount of detail and preparation that go into any presidential speech, it would be a safe wager that he knew he was not speaking the truth. The matter of monetary reimbursement was publicly stated by the American Medical Association within twenty-four hours. No doctor ever receives even $1,000 for the amputation of a foot. They also do not receive payment "immediately." The facts, according to the AMA, are that reimbursement for amputations are slow in coming and average between $500 and $700.

And then there was his own grandmother's hip replacement surgery, fully covered by her own insurance plan. He questioned whether it was necessary in light of her preexisting condition:

"I don't know how much that hip replacement cost," Obama said in the interview. "I would have paid out of pocket for that hip replacement just because she's my grandmother. You just get into some very difficult moral issues [when considering whether] to give my grandmother, or everybody else's aging grandparents or parents, a hip replacement when they're terminally ill. That's where I think you just get into some very difficult moral issues."[3]

So by his own thinking, and now admission, had it been left to a public option or single-payer government-run plan, there is a strong possibility she would have been denied coverage for her hip replacement because of her preexisting condition. But wasn't that one of the massively huge problems his public option plan was supposed to prevent? So is everyone else's granny supposed to die in misery with a crumbling, dysfunctional hip, just because they are sick with something else?

Is this the utopia that Obama's health care plan is supposed to usher in?

I wondered at the time if anyone besides me felt the least bit queasy about the fact that, in order to convince us and to show us the rightness of the system he proposed, the president had to resort to illustrations of unnecessary amputations?

Did his confusion between $500 and $50,000 cause anyone else who was struggling to pay their bills to shudder at his lack of clarity on the numbers in a system on which he wants to spend $3,000,000,000,000?

These are important questions, and I desperately hope that while he was vacationing that week in August at Martha's Vineyard, he worked in a little time to consider them.

TIME FOR A BIT OF CLARITY

There is a lost concept in the worldview of President Obama, and it is simply this: "the dignity of personhood."

How can a man who campaigned so persistently on the ideals of caring for one's brother care so little about the reputation of doctors, the welfare of his own grandmother, the innocent eyes and ears of children, and of course, the lives of innocent, unborn human beings?

For all of the frustrations that exist when it comes to the Obama administration's policies on the economy, national defense, and border security, one question underscores them all: does the individual have a fundamental right to life, and to self-determination?

In the mind of Barack Obama the answer is, "It depends." But the answer for common-sense America has always been, "Absolutely YES!"

The president actually believes that a person doesn't have a guaranteed right to life. Yet our founders secured that as the first of the three most important rights: "life, liberty, and the pursuit of happiness." They did so knowing that one built on the next. You cannot have liberty if you are not living, and the pursuit of happiness is difficult when you are not free.

Ultimately, friends, the views that we carry on the importance of protecting the innocent and vulnerable individual, tell us a great deal more about *all* of our social and fiscal issues than any other. For our founders believed that God guaranteed the right of all men to live. So much more important it becomes, then, for our president to believe the same!

CHAPTER
FIFTEEN

Re-creating Family: An All-Out Assault on Morality

During Thanksgiving weekend 2009, when Tiger Woods ran his SUV over a fire hydrant and then wrapped it around a neighborhood tree, few if any knew of the damage that would be done to his family in the following days. It turned out that the most successful golfer in history and his wife had been arguing over his repeated adultery. He had cheated on her with more than a dozen women, and more were being revealed with each news cycle.

Tiger caused terrible damage to his family and his reputation. Depressed and saddened, he withdrew to his gated community in the weeks that followed. There, behind the window shades of his home, he sought to examine his sinful nature, his ability to hurt those he loved, and to wonder if he would ever be able to get his life back together again.

Yet for all the agony that Woods's actions had caused his wife, children, endorsement clients, and fans, the scale of his actions paled in comparison to the merciless march the current administration was on at year's end. It would ruin the lives and finances of many families in America.

Every day that President Obama pushed for the government take-over of health care, he advocated injuring individuals and families by the thousands. Every time he contemplated the idea of spending trillions more of our tax dollars, he lessened his chances of reducing the un-/ underemployment rates that were drastically impacting one out of every five families. By refusing to seriously address the need for job creation, and by invoking ridiculous propositions such as "jobs saved," the president demonstrated a callousness not to one injured spouse, but to an aching nation.

If Tiger had put into practice a principle from my last book, *The Kind of Man Every Man Should Be*, and pursued reconciliation, forgiveness, and healthy life choices from that point on—all while agreeing to absolute accountability—he could have very well lost his wife and children anyway. Yet at the very least, by making such choices and by adopting a path different from the one that took him down the road of danger, Tiger could have given his children and possibly even his former wife a degree of health and sanity. This would not have replaced what betrayal had taken from them, but his desire to reconcile would've produced healthy results.

President Obama, from all appearances, is not interested in healthy results, and it appears that he will continue to lead American down a dangerous path by refusing to admit that his statist view of the world has any flaws in it whatsoever. He will dig in. He will give more speeches. He will possibly even accept more absurd awards on the world stage. He refuses to see what everyone else easily does, that his actions and his stubborn refusal to pivot are damaging the future of millions of people. The federal spending and debt are breaking records under this president.

Even further demonstration of his disconnection is his push for green energy. He still wishes to punitively hurt energy companies, prevent the discovery of new sources, and forcibly change the American people's behavior while taxing them record rates—all over global warming, a nonissue. Even those who originally put the ideas forward have been caught admitting that in e-mails to each other.

Tiger's only chance at redeeming his life and, somewhere far down the road, his game, is to choose to be a different person. He must volitionally make better choices, better friends, and cling to the real love of one woman. I personally believe that those tasks are made easier if he couples those choices with a genuine belief, faith, and trust in God. President Obama's chances at redemption are actually easier; all he must do is admit the truth and make a handful of different choices about policy. Had he wished to redeem his party's chances of avoiding serious losses in 2010, he could have specifically chosen to drop the public option in health care, ensure the prevention of any federal monies used for abortion, scrap "cap and trade," reject unbalanced budgets, and extend federal tax reductions for small businesses.

None of that would make him a conservative, or even a Republican, but it would demonstrate that he genuinely takes seriously the lives of those he serves.

And while his weekly poll numbers have fallen, it appears he has not yet suffered enough—nor sensed the suffering of the American people enough (just yet)—for him to take the serious steps that Tiger Woods was forced to take.

Because of this, "We the People" feel very much like the wife who has been cheated on and even abused by neglect, dishonesty, and trickery.

Thus the only question left to answer is, "Whose love and affection is the nation's president truly pursuing?"

FROM THE UNFAITHFUL TO THE PROFANE

The week ending March 28, 2010, was a fairly significant one, as the health care reform bill battle was on in Congress. Historic federal graft wasn't enough; groundbreaking requests were made by President Obama for a T-shirt with the "f" word emblazoned on it. (You remember when

Vice President Biden whispered in his ear what a big deal the signing of the Patient Protection and Affordable Care Act of 2010 [commonly referred to as Obamacare] was. And only days later, the president wanted a T-shirt bearing the sentiment.) Congressman Bart Stupak's drowning in his $52 million worth of requests for illegal pork for his district didn't suitably offend (primarily because he was paid off to abandon his conscience on the issue of abortion and dutifully support the president's health care bill on a purely partisan vote).

And all of it pointed to what I called at the time "the worst of Obamacare!" At least I hoped it was the worst. Who could actually know?

Certainly not Congress, because they didn't even read the bill. Nancy Pelosi informed us of this on a day now forever enshrined on YouTube. And for the few members who did read it, Sarah Palin's reference to keeping "Democrats in the [political] crosshairs" didn't quite go far enough.

But nestled in the mush that was the new health care reform law was something rotten: a failure to prevent Obamacare dollars from going to provide erectile dysfunction drugs for convicted pedophiles. Tom Coburn, the Senate's only medical doctor, warned us all that it could happen without an amendment to prevent it. But Obama didn't listen to him at his "all-faux-show" bipartisan conference, and the ultra-partisan Democrats showed Dr. Coburn the door over his request for such a common-sense amendment. Without it, there was no specific language to prevent Obamacare dollars from being used in such a fashion. So now, under federal law, because of lawmakers who defied you in voting the 2,700-page fiasco through to the president's desk, our tax dollars would provide sexual performance–enhancing drugs to convicted rapists, those who've committed sexual assault, and serial pedophiles.

Oddly enough, the president, not seeing this coming either, kept touting another lie all week: that Medicare would not be additionally burdened because private companies wouldn't be forced to dump employees into the Medicare program. But that was before people read the bill, and the real program was unveiled. Now we know that millions more people will be applying for Medicare funds than the president told us.

Obama and company have arrogantly mocked those who "distorted" the description of his takeover of the health insurance industry in America. And on one level I tend to agree. The distortion was grossly underestimated.

Since March 28, we have daily awakened only to find program after program, policy after policy, bribe after bribe, and dishonesty upon dishonesty in a bill that was supposed to balance the budget, be completely transparent, and lift Americans out from beneath the crushing costs of health care. Turns out, it was all a lie. Nary a piece of the legislation turned out to be what it was touted to be. But Viagra for child rapists . . . now, that's one I don't think anyone saw coming.

Except, of course, for Dr. Tom Coburn!

TIME FOR A BIT OF CLARITY

When the aftermath of the elections of 2010 was finally sorted out, few things had made voters angrier, according to the exit polling, than the willful stupidity of Obamacare. Needless regulation in areas where the patient's well-being was not considered on one hand, and ideas such as sex-enhancing drugs for convicted sex offenders on the other, appeared to be tremendously negligent at best.

Congress was doing the opposite of effecting true, beneficial change. Instead, our elected officials were cheaply, crassly, and nervously attempting to insert a new agenda, a Far Left, progressive agenda, into our national psyche.

Part of their success depended upon the citizens staying willfully removed from politics and the controversy it caused. But the balancing act that the Tea Party movement and others brought to the discussion educated and enlightened people, amplifying the thunderous roar of those who felt as though Washington was not listening.

The stage was set for the second half of President Obama's presidency. Would justice, small government, and integrity make a comeback?

CHAPTER SIXTEEN

Redefining Good and Evil

Barack Obama sometimes seems more boyish than manly. It's not that he is unwilling to open a door for his bride, or sit on the sofa and giggle with his daughters at the end of the day. These are some of his most endearing traits and ones he should be applauded for. But he is also a lost soul, a child who is haunted by shadows of absent fathers, a man who grew up in a confusing family dynamic, a social order that was changing drastically in the years of his maturing. He is also haunted by questions about God, faith, belief, and righteousness.

In the context of these confusions, apprehensions, frustrations, and constant adjustments, his winning smile, cheerful demeanor, and ability to glide through the day all became defense mechanisms that others have fed off of. Where once he lacked confidence, now he projects it. Where he lacks conviction, he rides on instinct. And occasionally, where he lacks an anchor, he follows his hunches. Sometimes it doesn't work out very well. It's a mixed bag, filled with some good, some dreadful. But it is his ability to continue to churn forward no matter the outcome that has propelled him to this point in life. Unfortunately, it is a rudderless path. He desires the world to be a place of utopic goodness, but he rejects the very reality that has kept society from being that since day one—the presence of sin. In doing so he deceives himself into believing that life is not lived on a scale of good or bad, but of attainability or achievability. And living a life without an effective and objective moral foundation puts people in very awkward conundrums. On several occasions in the first two years of the Obama presidency, this defective kink in the works would gum up the gears in more ways than one.

WHY "STUPID IS AS STUPID DOES"

If you're the leader of the free world, there may be a few things that take you by surprise from time to time. Big things, like planes flying into buildings of your largest city. Or sometimes not such big things, like reporters from your hometown asking you a question in a press conference.

One thing is for sure—these surprises will often tell everyone watching a little bit about who you really are. So if a reporter asks you a question that you probably shouldn't weigh in on, then it's just smart to say, "I have no comment on that at this time." But if you choose not to take that wiser course of action and instead actually *answer* questions on which you do not have the facts, then don't be blaming the media the next day, claiming that they are "distracting" the American people from the important issue. Most Americans believe that the integrity of the president of the United States is a fairly important issue.

The setting was the summer of 2009. It was late June when a professor at Harvard University, Henry Louis Gates, arrived at his home in Cambridge, Massachusetts, after a trip overseas. His front door was jammed, so he and his driver tried to force it open. In the dark of the evening, a concerned neighbor, not recognizing the men, dialed the

Cambridge police, and what happened next dominated the headlines of newspapers for the next few weeks. There were words exchanged between the officer, who is white, and the professor, who is black, and it ended in Dr. Gates's arrest for disorderly conduct. The professor claimed he was the victim of racial discrimination, while the police officer said that Dr. Gates had "exhibited loud and tumultuous behavior." The situation made its way to the attention of Lynn Sweet, longtime Chicago-based journalist, who asked the president about the incident at his next press conference

In his response, the president said that the Cambridge police had "acted stupidly," citing "a long history in this country of African-Americans . . . being stopped by law enforcement disproportionately."[1] The uproar that followed in the next few days was legitimate. The Cambridge police felt slighted, as did many police departments across the nation.

When it was demonstrated to the world that it had been Professor Gates who had been the primary cause of the kerfuffle, that the Cambridge police had acted with integrity, and that there was no wrong-doing by the public officials, President Obama called for his now famous "beer summit" to have a chat with the two gentlemen to straighten it all out. He invited the two men to the White House, where they could have a few beers together and talk.

We could probably justify Obama's misstep by observing that it had been a hard week, that the plans over which he had labored long hours (universal government-sponsored health care) were twisting in the wind, and that his own horrible performance in his press conference had left him so exhausted that he simply dropped his guard for the final question. But if that is true, then the first thing that should have happened the following morning was a publicly issued apology for tying the Cambridge Police Department to, in Obama words, "the long history of racial profiling."[2] He should've also on some level taken ownership and admitted that he was the one who "acted stupidly" in accusing the Cambridge police of the same. But for the ruthlessly pragmatic Obama, it would go against nature to do so.

RUTHLESSLY PRAGMATIC "FAITH"

Since many believe that faith is an effective way to deal with right and wrong, good and evil, just and unjust, in life, it is particularly discouraging to observe how President Obama views faith in general. Fundamentally, President Obama believes that there is little difference in the faiths that people hold. The basis for this, in his mind, comes from a lack of conviction in his own faith, and therefore the assumption is easily transferred to those of other faiths as well.

During his time in office in the Senate, he claimed to have replaced attending a local church with the reading of little messages sent to him on his BlackBerry. Evidently God now has an app, and as such, can easily fit in his pocket. Obama still has infamously not found or consistently attended a church in the Washington, D.C., area at the time of this writing, nearly twenty-four months into his term.

Digging further on his lack of belief, however, if we are to understand him from his own explanations: The last church he did attend was pastored by Dr. Jeremiah Wright. This was the same Afrocentric, racist "brother of the cloth" that President Obama later denounced in his run for presidency. He denounced him for supposedly beginning to spout a whole new line of racist rhetoric, flat-out lies, and distortions that, while Obama "attended" faithfully for twenty years, Wright had somehow kept hidden from him up to that point.

Wright must have kept those core convictions from Obama while Wright was mentoring the young family man, baptizing his two daughters, and acting as their family pastor. Yet if we are to understand Obama correctly, either he had never heard Wright's racism preached from the pulpit, or somehow, in all the meaningful mentoring talks in which they had engaged since young Obama moved to Chicago, Wright had avoided discussing them. I find both hard to believe since there is videotape of Wright screaming the garbage at the top of his lungs.[3]

As mentioned previously, Obama has told the Muslim world that America shares their values. But female subjugation, stoning to death women who have been raped, and even female genital mutilation have nothing to do with American values.

And in a radio address to the nation on April 3, 2010, the president did it again. Either he showed a lack of recognition that faiths are all different, or he purposefully intended to make them "the same," drawing them all into, not the family of God, but the "family of man."

Obama wants little of organized faith to be present in today's national culture. Oh, sure, getting the little first daughters all decked out in their new Easter dresses and letting them scurry for eggs on the White House lawn is fun and all, but anything more "faith-based" than that and we're going to have problems. I can only assume that it was for reasons such as these that he did not merely refuse to attend a White House National Day of Prayer and Remembrance in 2009; he canceled it.

Those people of faith are the ones causing all the problems, after all. They don't trust his government schemes because they'd prefer to keep more of their own dollars and be able to give more generously to the missions and causes they believe in. They don't trust his view of caring for the "least of these"[4] because every time the president attempts to, it creates worsening conditions for those who are the least. They don't trust his view of what is sacred, because President Obama believes it's somehow moral to allow a born infant to die of starvation on the shelf of a soiled utility closet in a hospital named "Christ" (Christ Hospital, Oak Lawn, Illinois).

People of faith don't trust the president's view of morality because he desires to put homosexuals in the same barracks with straight soldiers. Yet he seems to think that men lockering with women would be a problem. They don't trust his judgment because he seems to trust others whose judgment is not even debatable, such as Rev. Wright, Iran's Ahmedinejad, and Venezuelan dictator Hugo Chavez. He also openly defies the sound judgment of our allies—including Israel.

Mr. President, there is a world of difference between the moral code of Islam and that of Jews and Christians.

Even the debate between Judaism and Christianity is an important one, as the two groups couldn't be farther apart on the fundamental understandings of redemption, the Messiah, and what is to come. Our president's attempt to sweep it all together and tie it up with a bow is dishonest.

Toward the end of that April 3 radio address, the president claimed that religious faith had been openly practiced in every corner of the world for thousands of years. In doing so he implied that nothing could stop the free exercise of faith, and that free exercise of religion is not unique to the American concept rooted in the first amendment. Yet President Obama knows this simply isn't true. Just ask any Jew what happened to their people in Germany during World War II. And for the better part of seventy years throughout the Soviet bloc of nations, the same could be said for genuine Christianity. And in many ways this exact persecution continues in Somalia, the Sudan, sub-Saharan Africa, much of Asia, and the Middle and Far East.

So, President Obama's assertions in that radio address were either grotesquely ignorant or purposefully dishonest. As to which it was, I leave that for him to answer.

TIME FOR A BIT OF CLARITY

There are many in conservative circles who strongly disagree with what I'm about to say because they believe it to be a fundamentally flawed view. I cannot disagree with them any more strongly!

The genuine difference between the Right and the Left is not their view of government size, taxes, national defense, abortion, homosexuality, the environment, terrorism, border security, Supreme Court nominees, or even the Tea Party. Neither is it prescribed by which television networks they watch or whether they are fans of Bill O'Reilly or Keith Olbermann. It is not whether they watch or listen to the Kevin McCullough show or *The Rachel Maddow Show*. The real difference is far simpler than all of these.

The primary difference between the Left and the Right is their view of God. To the *Right*, God is someone who is outside of humanity, uncontrollable by human effort, beyond them, sovereign over them. Whether we are talking about observant Jews, Orthodox, Roman Catholics, mainline Protestants, charismatics, or evangelical Christians, to people on the right, God is an authority in their lives, who guides their actions, calls them to repentance, and seeks to mold them into better people, with greater integrity, who ultimately impact their world.

To the *Left*, God is someone who might not exist. Or if he does, he is relatively uninvolved or uninterested and certainly unauthoritative in today's world. He might be controlled by human intent. He may even be able to be squelched altogether. But generally speaking, he is unwanted, unneeded, or needed on the terms of what the person desires, not what true omnipotence would logically require.

If a person is confused by moral order—if he or she believes that good is sometimes bad, bad is sometimes good, wrong is sometimes right, and right is many times wrong—then that individual demonstrates a lack of moorings on the issue of an authoritative God. And if God is not an authority, then he's a pet, or a pixie, or a playmate . . . but he's not important.

By this simple grid being laid over the life span of Barack Obama we learn a few things.

His tough transitional childhood living with a mother who raised him for some years with a Muslim Indonesian, gave him up to be raised by culturally "Christian" grandparents, and left him to go to university more or less an atheist, before turning to an atheistic "liberation theology" in adult life, has left President Obama afloat on the most fundamental questions of all time. Therefore it should not be surprising that his own radar of right versus wrong is confused, misaligned, and sometimes malfunctioning. It's how he was raised.

And a word to us on this point: It matters how we raise our children. It matters if they have two parents. It matters if they have a father who is present. The instruction in faith that you give your children *matters*. And it matters how you train and shape their conscience.

PART FOUR

Accountability
to Caesar

CHAPTER
SEVENTEEN

Context for Credibility

Over my span of years on-air as a talk show host, I have attempted to drive one clear thought home every time I have been asked about the overreach and power grabs of government: we don't work for the government; they work for us!

We the People of this great nation are not subjects to a ruling class. We are not held back from accomplishing that toward which we truly set our hearts, simply because we were born to a given station in life. And we certainly do not have to bend the knee and bow at the altar of a monarch, whether he believes himself an agent of God or not. We the People in fact *are* the rulers of our nation, and as such we must consider the most sanctified form of self-determining government ever invented.

When asked about this from a faith-based context, many of the Christians who interact with me say, "But wait a second; what does the Bible say about the authority of those who govern?" (Many times referring to Hebrews 13:17.) In asking such a question, these well-intentioned people reveal that they fundamentally do not understand the power structure or chain of command in America. Simply stated, President Barack Obama is not a king, nor does he deserve the royal treatment that royalty would be entitled to by bloodline. He is not a dictator, with absolute ability to impose his will upon those he considers his subjects. He is not a tyrant with absolute power to use for any purpose he sees fit.

In fact, our presidents all have more in common with the night manager at McDonald's than with any of those analogies. Because simply put, they, including President Obama, are employees, not rulers. And to believe anything more than that about the position causes us to misunderstand our role in our nation. It also allows those who serve in government to believe themselves to be something more than humble servants.

In the New Testament scriptures, Jesus is asked about civil authority and the obligation to observe it. His answer: "Render to Caesar the things that are Caesar's, and to God the things that are God's" (Mark 12:17 ESV).

Those to whom He spoke these words marveled at what He meant, but the short of it is pretty simple. "Do your duty" in the civic arena—as it is in keeping with God's agenda, and beyond that, obey God in all things. So we as citizens have a duty to vote, to be involved in the process, and to know the issues. For We the People are the board of directors, and it is our responsibility to write sound laws, elect qualified representatives, and if necessary, run for office ourselves—in order that we might effect a true, just, and good society.

When we elect presidents, senators, or House representatives, we should think of them in different dynamics than we presently do. They are candidates interviewing for positions for which *we* are doing the hiring. And should they get the job, there must be a constant reminder that they can be terminated from their positions. We have no obligation to "support" or "oppose" anyone mindlessly. But we have every expectation to hold them accountable for all that they do on our watch, in our house (the White House is known as "the People's House"), and on our dime.

THE VERY REAL PROBLEM OF OBAMANIA AND SYCOPHANTASIA

In September 2009, a handful of the president's supporters garnered large headlines. They had one thing in common: They were rabid supporters of President Obama, and in many ways reflected his very own tendencies and lack of candor, but with far less grace.

They openly confessed to murder, they had refused to allow independent investigations to look into their questionable activities, they had pledged retribution toward those who exposed them, and they had even proudly told a creeped-out nation that they would do it all over again. Unfortunately for the president, they were a precise example of the type of political worldview that swept him into office.

Over the last two weeks of August into September's early weeks, two courageous young people (Hannah Giles and James O'Keefe—otherwise known as "the pimp and the prostitute") did the nation a favor by accomplishing something the media establishment, the president, and Congress would not. Through the simple act of asking questions, these two twenty-somethings produced perhaps the most effective sting operation ever performed against a crooked organization seeking to rot society through its own diseased corruption. As a result, the evidence produced forced both houses of Congress to vote to stop all funding to the group.

On the videotapes seen 'round the world, ACORN workers, literally from sea to shining sea, advised fraud, bragged about murder, and confessed to their own past operations of prostitution agencies. Some of them, including the self-proclaimed killer, lauded the current administration as being able to "get things done."[1]

But how did the head of this supposedly honorable organization respond? By falsely accusing Fox News of setting the whole thing up, and pledging to take hard-core legal action against the two-person team that captured the wrongdoing on tape. Then, when questioned directly on *Fox News Sunday*, the head of ACORN refused to say she would allow outside investigators to look into ACORN's vetting and operations practices (again, all the while singing the president's praises).

Then in the final week of September 2009, a videotape turned up from a Burlington, New Jersey, public elementary school in which the children were the ones singing literal praise and worship tunes to the president. Crooning about his "great accomplishments" in making the "economy number one again" and replacing the name of the crucified Lord with the name of President Obama were just some of the elements of the tape.[2]

Nearly everyone in the nation described the event as creepy and inappropriate, and even liberal trolls on conservative blogs were referring to the tape as "scary." Everyone except the principal of the school where the event took place, that is. I personally phoned the school within hours of the tape's controversy coming to light late one September morning. The administrator's office told me that they

- would not acknowledge the tape's existence
- would not confirm or deny that parents had been notified prior to the "worship" service
- would not confirm if children who felt uncomfortable had been allowed an alternate activity

What the school gladly told me was how they had knowledge of an "illegal tape" that had been made and distributed of a "private class activity." As contradictory as that sounds, that is what they *did* ultimately admit. As if to assume that people did not have a right to know every last jot and tittle of what happens in that school at any given moment.

After twenty-four hours, the school finally acknowledged the tape's existence and did express outrage . . . at those who were complaining and calling the school to voice their opinion. As it turned out, the person who likely made the recording, and who was definitely the first person to upload it to the Web, was a classmate of President Obama at Harvard, and as it turns out, a friend of the principal of this elementary school—both of whom were ardent supporters of the president.

Once the jig was up, the principal finally took questions from parents, whom she reportedly told that she had "no regrets about how the matter was handled," and that she would "do it again," exactly the same way.[3]

I understand clearly that these are not the average voter who decided late in the game to support President Obama. I know that many Independents who initially voted for him regret their votes, and stories like this make them cringe even worse at the reality of what their votes did. But these are the types of people who are energized and currently *work* for this president. He has surrounded himself with people who have this type of character for the entirety of his political life.

And my best hunch is, if these ardent supporters see the president befriend many of our nation's enemies (Chavez, Qaddafi), offer nothing more serious than more talk of sanctions to radicals bent on our destruction (Iran, North Korea), and curtly side against our friends in significant conflicts of their own (Honduras, Israel, Poland, Czech Republic) . . . if he is willing to tell the American people one thing to get elected, and then without so much as batting an eye, embark on the most radical transformation of America in our history . . .

What's to keep those who sing worship songs to him from thinking they can do the same exact things in their own spheres of influence?

It's just how he "gets things done!"

LOSING AMERICA, DIRECTLY AND QUICKLY

When two hundred Hispanic students skipped class from Live Oak High School in May of 2010 and marched through downtown Morgan Hill,

California, chanting "Si, se puede" (loosely translated "Yes, we can") intermixed with "We want respect," none were banned from school attendance on their return. But when five students, one of them an American from Latino roots, wore American flags to school as a sign of patriotic speech, they were labeled "incendiary." They were instructed to turn their shirts inside out to cover up the American flag. And when they refused to surrender their First Amendment right to expression, they were given unexcused absences.

Assistant principal Miguel Rodriguez called the flag-draped wardrobe "incendiary" because the students had chosen to wear them on May 5, popularly known as Cinco de Mayo. This date celebrates Mexico's defeat of the French in the Battle of Pueblo (in a war that Mexico lost a year later).

The school's administration went further in claiming the five students were attempting "to start a fight" and "adding fuel to the fire." Some Latino parents chimed in and chided the five students, one of whom is of Mexican ethnic heritage, saying, "We're all offended by it." One parent, Teresa Casillas, claimed that her Hispanic children were upset by the behavior of the boys wearing the flagged shirts, calling it disrespectful.

Yet for all the outcry, not an ounce of proof has erupted that the boys made any actions of provocation—except wear the shirts on Cinco de Mayo.

One of the more ignorant utterances by one of the Hispanic student protestors summed up the stupidity best: "It's disrespectful to do it on Cinco de Mayo," said Jessica Cortez, a Live Oak sophomore. "They can be a patriot on some other day. Not that specific day."[4]

And so this is what the argument has been reduced to. Cinco de Mayo is not even celebrated en masse by ethnic Mexicans living in Mexico. It's mostly celebrated in Pueblo itself and here in the United States. Yet some of the militant Latinos living in Morgan Hill are exhibiting symptoms of a problem that is widespread. Their entitlement mentality not only flouts our laws, but has now led to limiting the most legitimate expression of freedom: patriotism.

This, however, was a small eruption compared to the issues that stemmed from a hostile Obama administration opposing the elected leaders and voters of the state of Arizona in the first two years of the administration. It was bad enough that the Obama administration went on a systematic campaign to discredit the state of Arizona, whose citizens voted into law the right to reinforce federal guidelines for immigration. The lies were widely told and never retracted by news agencies that should have known better. It was worse when tens of thousands of illegals marched on downtown streets without any fear to demand socialized redistribution of rights to those who are not citizens and who disrespect the laws of our nation.

Normally, I'm exceedingly compassionate to all people groups who wish to get to America. After all, if they wish to change their allegiance, support the values of our nation, and identify with the cause of what is true, just, and good, then they should, in fact, be ideal candidates for American citizenship.

Constantly we are told by media and "immigration rights activists" (read, "open border apologists") that America is a big enough nation to be able to handle a significant increase in immigration. This is a notion I'm not totally in disagreement with. Yet there is nothing unconstitutional, unlawful, immoral, or even unkind about asking those who come here to identify who they are, and state the lawful basis they have for coming through our border gate.

The actions of the two-hundred students of Morgan Hill marching on the streets—though repulsive in its intent—are constitutionally protected expression. So were the actions of five students who wore American flag shirts.

It may be the expression du jour to blame America for the ills of all that goes wrong in the world. Pardon me if I don't. Principal Boden and assistant principal Rodriguez should be fired from Live Oak High School in Morgan Hill, California. The school board could do so easily. And if they needed to be politically correct about what they call it, merely label it a permanent unexcused absence.

The families of los Estados Unidos deserve much better!

TIME FOR A BIT OF CLARITY

When the president allowed his Justice Department to take on Governor Jan Brewer and the voters of the state of Arizona, he believed he was assisting his administration in winning over minority Hispanic voters for the cause of the Democrat Party in the elections of 2010. This was a notion that got bounced on its head the night of November 2, 2010. But there is a larger issue at play in the unfolding of the disturbing principles behind these actions. For whether it's the constituency that elected him, or the not-yet-legal residents living within our borders, the Obama administration has consistently mirrored a similar problem in his approach to foreign policy.

In his mind President Obama considers himself a citizen of the world first, and a citizen of America second. Fundamentally, this is a different way of viewing the office, the nation, and the voters than what we've ever experienced before. Because of this, voters cannot be confident that President Obama—in day-to-day discussions, and even large-issue policy decisions—is viewing the potential viable solutions from a viewpoint of what benefits America first.

No matter who the president is, this should never be the case. American presidents have a different responsibility toward their passions, their loyalties, and their responsibilities than any other American citizen for the simple reason that they are citizen number one in their individual administrations.

An American president is to be an advocate for and a defender of this nation at all costs, under all circumstances, for the entirety of his or her duration in office. Put another way, none of us as a CEO would hire an employee who worries that one of our competitors may not like the decision he or she was about to make. No coach would put a player in the game if the player asked, "Will the other team's fans like me if I throw this pass for a touchdown against them?" Presidents *have* to be loyal, before all other loyalties, to America. It's what we've hired them to do. To be. And to expect. In evaluating our hiring practices, every two, four, or six years, we should be mindful of this. And we should never forget that we *have the right* to poke and prod any candidate for that job that we feel may be suspect on the matter.

CHAPTER EIGHTEEN

Getting Things Right?

"Kevin, do you honestly believe that everything this president does is wrong—even dangerous? Do you really believe with all your heart that he is beyond hope?" A caller began a recent conversation on my morning show with these questions. But it's not as though I haven't heard them before. Hundreds of times in the course of a decade, people have asked me similar questions. "Are liberals always bad?" "Do progressives always want America to fail?" "Do you like anyone who ever thinks differently than you?" Different questions but all leading to the same answer, and seeking the same honest response: Can progressives get anything right?

The short reply is, "Well, yes, perhaps, but only as they understand, respond, and act as a conservative."

I don't believe there are lots of different, morally equal ways of standing on issues. I honestly believe there are answers that are rooted in moral truth, and those that aren't. Progressives *need* a world that has fifty thousand shades of grey. But ultimately the world doesn't—especially if things are going to improve.

The world is not a better place if all of us are partially rotten, and getting more partially rotten each day. Not at all. The world will be a better place if all of us know where we are rotten and begin to address and change those things about ourselves as quickly as we possibly can. Acceptance of rotting souls isn't love. Love is the refusal to let someone stay in the rotting condition to begin with, no matter how hard it is to get that person to move from the rot.

TIGER WOODS, BRIT HUME, AND PRESIDENT OBAMA

In an earlier chapter we highlighted Tiger Woods and his fall from grace. He seems to be moving himself out of his formerly rotten ways. In one of the more bizarre seasons of criticism to be laid at the feet of a pundit, former Fox News chief Brit Hume did a rare thing the first week of January 2010. He offered a strikingly personal and profoundly, sincerely held belief concerning Woods's future. His opinion was not welcomed by major players across the American media spectrum, but the advice he proffered to the World's Greatest Golfer would be well heeded by the World's Most Powerful Leader.

Brit's advice was met even by unease on the set of the Fox News program on which he suggested that Tiger Woods might find lasting forgiveness and peace by turning to Christianity (what he would later revise in additional media appearances to actually mean "turning to Jesus Christ" personally).

There was much more at play than the initial glance at the incident revealed. Those who have criticized Hume are mopes. For if an average citizen cannot truly suggest where another hurting human being may actually be able to find hope, what is, in fact, left of real America?

Tiger is a man without a father, for his passed away a few years ago. He would likely benefit from the advice of a decent man. Brit Hume is characterized by those from the Left and Right as one of the most principled individuals to ever work in network news. Yet when you consider his circumstances, his position, and how lost President Obama genuinely is, he would benefit equally if not more than Tiger by turning to the person of Jesus Christ.

President Obama is also a fatherless father who dotes on his children. But on governing this nation he is in way over his head. And without some sort of sharp correction, he will not only create a damning future for his own daughters, but for the whole of the rest of the nation.

Brit Hume retired notably. His achievements were visible for all to see. He did accomplish as much as he could in pioneering the way news was reported, particularly from Washington, D.C. And his spirited debates and observations on election nights or even Supreme Court cases were always worth staying up for. There was a reason for that. As a principled journalist, recognized by the Left and Right as a man of deep personal integrity and the highest personal standards of professionalism, he proved that a journalist could tell the news of the day and *not* sell his or her soul in the process—the very essence of which is exactly what Tiger and President Obama are missing.

In life it doesn't really matter if you attain the highest heights if in the process of doing so you lose your wife, your family, your children, or you destroy the world into which your children will grow. What matters is not who in this world likes you, but whether God is satisfied with your condition. It is not so much about being popular in the eyes of your fellow human beings as much as it is about character. And on this note I believe President Obama has a mixed scorecard. Yes, his policies in large measure have devastated the country, so much so that he lost record numbers of party members in the midterm elections.

Yet for the sake of balance, I don't want anyone reading this text to think that I believe that President Barack Obama is a condemned man and cursed to a netherworld of existence in which the best that can be hoped for is a sort of neutral incapacitation. To that end I want to highlight a couple of areas where I think the president set the right tone, lived the right example, and should be recognized for his diligence, commitment, and steadfastness.

You can see it in his love and affection for his wife, Michelle. His desire to be a good husband, to dote on her in public, to cherish his time with her on date nights, and to heed her input on preparing their family for runs at public office demonstrate a degree of integrity for the communication and importance of his home life.

Much the same could be said of his love for his daughters. President Obama has time and again said that his favorite time of day is when he is able to put the nation away for the night and just be with the daughters, as a family, a loving father laughing with, talking to, and listening to the hearts of his precious girls.

Our nation faces grave circumstances. On President Obama's watch no fewer than seven terror attacks have been unleashed against us on our own turf. Yet the lack of seeing or distinguishing right from wrong (the very essence of personal integrity) has prevented the president from protecting us, whereas he would defend to the death his own daughters' welfare.

President Obama would do well to heed the advice of Brit Hume. And oddly enough, I believe that Hume, regardless of who he voted for, would find himself very much at ease relaying to the president why a committed walk with Jesus Christ might just be the most life-changing thrill he could ever experience. In fact, I challenge President Obama to invite Mr. Hume to the people's house and see for himself. I think both Brit and Jesus are totally up to the task!

BUT HE EVEN GOT POLICY STUFF RIGHT ONCE TOO

Following the BP oil spill in the Gulf, President Obama decided to initially take a risky step in the right direction for the nation's energy future.

Make that twenty-seven risky steps.

Sure, his supporters will attempt to hammer him for it, and the reality of taking the necessary action has made his secretary of the interior, Ken Salazar, look foolish and out of the loop, but none of this should negate the good that will come of President Obama's pro-drilling actions. To be specific, following the *Deepwater Horizon* oil rig explosion on April 20,

2010, the administration has granted oil and gas companies twenty-seven exemptions from doing in-depth environmental studies of oil exploration in the Gulf of Mexico.

After the disaster the president assured some that there was an immediate moratorium on any offshore drilling. At least that's what his supporters thought they heard him say. What the president specifically promised was a "relentless response effort to stop the leak and prevent more damage to the Gulf."[1] And it is true—he did end up shutting down four thousand platform rigs for a period of time.

Fortunately, even Obama's Interior Department believes that further exploration and even drilling can occur safely, and that as tragic as April 20 was, it must not be allowed to be the end of our search for energy independence (especially in our waters, off our shores, in our territories).

That is exactly what our position should be!

It makes no sense to retreat into an imaginary cave, believing that all drilling efforts will result in similar events. In recent years we have been increasingly apprised of our own natural energy resources, those that fall within our own control. It is actually a sign of irresponsibility for an administration to not leverage every available resource to uncap those stores and to remove the pressure from our relationships with Islamic tyrants who profit from our purchase of oil from the Middle East.

Quickly the opposition to the president's decision to issue the twenty-seven exemptions reached fevered insanity. Peter Galvin of the Center for Biological Diversity complained, "Is there a moratorium on offshore drilling or not? Possibly the worst environmental disaster in U.S. history has occurred and nothing appears to have changed."[2]

Actually, Mr. Galvin, you're mistaken; something has changed, something responsible and good for America—the extension of our energy exploration to give us greater security, lower energy costs, and an overall sense of well-being for our citizens.

Galvin went further, "It looks to me like they're misleading the public."[3]

Yet, Mr. Galvin, it is the Department of the Interior who has granted the exemptions and revealed to the media that they've done so. How is that misleading?

Everyone in the nation expected the environmental extremists to harp on the oil spill as a reason to stop safe exploration for energy. Fortunately, and you know how rarely I find myself in this position, I am supporting President Obama for having the clarity to do the right thing and to keep the commitment and search for domestic energy sources alive.

Come to think of it, make that twenty-seven right things.

TIME FOR A BIT OF CLARITY

If conservatives, Christians, and others who in broad measure oppose the agenda of the Obama administration wish to be viewed as fair, then it is important for us to realize that kudos for what is done right will build us as much credibility in the eyes of those who are yet unconvinced than only criticizing that which has failed.

It is in no way disloyal to conservatism, Christianity, the Republican Party, the Tea Party, or any party to give compliments and credits where they are due. In fact, even if you disagree on everything else, giving praise for a job well done will be like "apples of gold in a setting of silver" (Proverbs 25:11 ESV). Put another way . . . you can catch more flies with honey!

CHAPTER
NINETEEN

Purposeful Dependency Ushers in Powerful Domestic Deception

In President Obama's ultimate ruthlessly pragmatic view toward national change, there is plenty of evidence about how President Obama responds to crises, tests, and the unexpected. It reveals to us a considerable amount concerning the character and integrity he embraces when attempting to problem solve. Or should it be said, the *lack thereof*?

Certainly there has been no single "I did not have sexual relations with that woman" moment. But in ways that far outweigh that felony committed by President Clinton, the Obama administration has systematically deceived and covered up, and in some cases, not very well.

From the smallest things, like omitting the words "their Creator" when reciting the Declaration of Independence, to the largest, like the matter of the Black Panthers' interference with voters on Election Day, the deceptions of Obama personally, as well as his cabinet, Congress, and party, have broken new territory.

This is explainable in part because his stay in the White House, the good graces of voters' minds, and the presidency all depend upon the voters believing a certain outcome. The more that President Obama is capable of causing the average person to believe that he or she needs him to be *in* the White House for certain benefits to stay in effect, the better off he is.

The more voters see themselves as entrepreneurs, capable of achieving great things without the government's involvement, the worse it gets for the political party that preaches such dependency. But for Obama it has been the sleeves-rolled-up intensity in some of the questionable activity that is causing even party loyalists to scratch their heads and hope he knows what he's doing.

And this was seen in spades in the elections of 2010.

MONKEYING AROUND IN THE ELECTIONS

There were at least three prominent races in which the White House directly involved itself in the campaign cycle of 2010. A strict adherence to the rules of campaigning and electioneering prevent such activity. But with the Democratic Party in charge of both houses of Congress, it was never a realistic possibility that there would be any type of federal proceedings to investigate the activity.

In the U.S. Senate Democratic primary races in Pennsylvania and Colorado, followed up by a last-ditch effort in the general election U.S. Senate race in Florida, President Barack Obama followed similar patterns: recruit, dissuade, replace.

The recruit was President Bill Clinton. His job was to dissuade the candidate not of Obama's preference from running for the particular race. Once the person had stepped aside, his replacement would help Obama accomplish the agenda. All three times Obama failed to displace the original party. The results were usually exposed, and the enormous landslide in election 2010 wrote off to irrelevancy any question as to whether his evil plan would've worked or not.

With such poor execution no wonder the results were ineffective. Consider the Democratic Senate primary race in Pennsylvania: It's hard to square the narrative on the White House's influence on the Democratic Senate Primary Race in Pennsylvania for 2010. For more than ten weeks, Mr. Joe Sestak ran his primary campaign on the notion that he was on the outs with the White House. He was independent. He was a man that Pennsylvanians could "trust" because he was "willing to stand up even to the President."[1]

For more than two months, he continually bragged about how he turned down a "job" offered to him by the White House to drop out of the Senate primary against Arlen Specter, Obama's favored candidate. It is illegal for the executive branch to interfere with an election, so if they did offer him a job in exchange for him standing down, that would be a felony, according to U.S. Code § 600.[2]

As the media continued to ponder the issue, the questions flourished. The White House attempted to brush under the rug any independent look into the matter, and Americans began to perk up their ears on what the potential conflict might be. And as the White House officials promised an explanation, the same day they were lunching with President Clinton, who fewer than twenty-four hours later would be implicated in the controversy, something truly began to stink.

Of course, given enough time behind closed doors, people can invent a narrative to suit their purposes. And by issuing that narrative and not allowing White House spokespersons to veer from it, they could help "control" the story on a Friday afternoon before a major holiday—the narrative in this situation being that former president Clinton had been the one to "make the offer," thereby excluding the White House directly from any implications.

Like so many careless things this president and his team had done politically, it seems the sloppy cleanup job of the Sestak mess quickly got messier than the oil spill in the gulf, and for good reasons. The story Sestak told for weeks on the campaign trail was very different from the "official" report released by the White House on that Friday. Pulling in Bill Clinton, one of the best-documented liars in elective political history, to be the fall guy was an easy way out. But their explanation didn't seem all that credible.

More questions began to emerge: Why did the White House Memo refer to discussions—plural—if the story is that President Clinton had only one contact with Sestak? Why didn't the White House Memo clearly state that no job was, in fact, offered to Sestak quid pro quo? Did not the leaving of this large loophole in the middle of their own explanation allow them the legal room to maneuver even more if the public pressure became hotter? And most damning of all, if the explanation was as simple as a call from Bubba to Pennsylvania Joe, why couldn't U.S. secretary of defense Robert Gates have answered that question from the press when he was asked daily for a period of weeks as to the specifics of what had happened? Defense Secretary Gates had been repeatedly asked if Joe Sestak, a retired admiral, had been considered for the highest position a naval officer could be granted, secretary of the navy. These questions were not satisfactorily answered by what many in the legal field were now calling the "whitewash memo" from the White House.

The final portion of this narrative, "It's not really criminal anyway, after all, it's only a misdemeanor,"[3] is the least satisfying portion of this entire saga. Nevertheless, this was the exact meme that the administration ended up playing repeatedly.

Pennsylvania voters most likely felt as though they've been dealt with quite dirty. At the very minimum, clear evidence existed that the White House did indeed attempt to influence their choices and manipulate the outcome of a Senate race. And an attempt to use his bully pulpit and all the resources that come with it demonstrated that President Obama would use his power in a corruptive way to generate an outcome of his—not the voters'—choosing.

The fact that Rahm Emanuel and Bill Clinton were also attached to this story only increases the likelihood of monkey business. After all, it was these two characters who took great delight fifteen years earlier in putting the legal system through tortured distortions of things as trite as what the word "is" is.

The voters of Pennsylvania deserved to know the entire set of facts, and they demanded that their own state conduct an independent investigation, whether the feds chose to look into it or not. If it had turned up nothing, then they may have had the confidence to vote for Sestak in November without fear. But the investigation did not happen, the suspicion remained, and Sestak went down in embarrassing defeat.

Breaking laws is not the only way to injure a hurting nation. Acting unethically is not always the same thing as acting illegally. But whether or not what the White House did was a felony, misdemeanor, or a legal act, there can be no dispute that Americans were thwarted, and that maleficent political action was in large measure rejected on November 2, 2010.

A TENACIOUS LADY ON THE WORST COVER-UP TO DATE

Megyn Kelly of Fox News has broken some big stories. But perhaps the most important story is one that runs right to the core of our American life. Her willingness to put on-air J. Christian Adams, a former attorney for the Department of Justice who had resigned his post in order to expose the racism inherent in the department, serves all of America extremely well.

Kelly's show was able to uncover that the Obama Department of Justice, headed by Eric Holder, had issued an edict that would prevent the department from prosecuting voter intimidation cases in which the victims were white and the intimidators were black. It was a policy, in effect, that promoted racism and set the guidelines that voter discrimination would be overlooked by the administration. The exclusive story should have been front-page news for the major newspapers and top-of-the-hour feeds for the 24/7 newsers. Four days after her original exclusive interview, a highly rated fellow Fox broadcaster, Glenn Beck, finally provided the first corollary coverage. Yet the *New York Times*, the *Washington Post*, CNN, MSNBC, and all the major networks still have yet to pen their first word of coverage.

Had Kelly been covering the dismissal of a case against two Ku Klux Klan members, every paper in America would've pinged it. Further, had the Justice Department issued an edict to ignore any further cases of voter intimidation by whites in which the victims were black, riots would've broken out in most of the nation's urban centers. Kelly endured pathetic treatment from the Department of Justice on the matter. She—along with J. Christian Adams, Mr. Beck, myself, and my morning listeners—have been slimed as racist for relaying some of the basic information she has brought to light.

Kelly left the morning slot on Fox in 2009 to give birth to her newborn. When she returned, she was awarded the afternoon solo gig that has dominated its ratings time slot. In a media environment where facts are often ignored, twisted, or run over roughshod, Megyn Kelly's tenacity in knowing, properly understanding, and relaying the factual information in the stories she features is without question. Talk to pundits on either side of the political spectrum and they will confirm that though she does not always ask them the questions they want to answer, they are unable to fault her personally.

In other words, Kelly does what good journalists have always done.

The biggest scandal to date in the Obama administration is his own Justice Department's edict to enforce a racist and discriminatory policy against Americans based on the skin color of the parties involved. It is a scandal that Eric Holder should be brought before Congress to answer for, as should all of the political appointees who played a hand in the decision.

It's disgusting to see Kelly treated in such a way. But something tells me that Megyn's tough enough to handle it.

TIME FOR A BIT OF CLARITY

The problem with government being able to get away with overt deception is not so much the issue that they try, but the fact that We the People allow them to succeed.

It really is not possible these days to put a value to someone who ruthlessly pursues the truth the way a Megyn Kelly does. These many months later, after the initial stories aired, the government is conducting its own internal investigation into the issues that J. Christian Adams revealed about specific behaviors within the Department of Justice and the Obama White House's attempts to shut down the debate, the dissent, the investigation, and the lasting outcome of the inquiry.

Journalism was at one time in this nation a loyal opposition to the government, asking the questions officials did not wish to be asked. The press did so in order to achieve the most transparent understanding of how the government was operating.

With few journalists doing their job anymore, it is incumbent upon us to take on citizen journalist roles. We are the ones who must seek, prod, dig, and discern. We must do so in order to get the best answers to the questions we have so that we can make the most sound decisions in our future hiring of civil servants.

There is more we can do as well, however. We can encourage a whole new generation of journalists to take the place of the ones who refuse to do their job. Megyn Kelly can lead the way as the new voice of journalism in America. I think our nation as a whole would be better off if she was, as opposed to say, Katie Couric.

CHAPTER TWENTY

Frozen Paralysis Kills Americans

Few things are less tasteful than arrogance among the empowered. Few things are sillier than believing one's own praise. Few people are more misguided than those who teach false doctrine, and few are more dangerous than those who willfully deceive in order to gain power.

On all four points President Obama stands head and shoulders above us all.

It seems, however, that he saves his ugliest bits of guile, disdain, and self-exaltation for when he is forced to deal with the American people. For as much as he would like to believe it, he is not higher than us, but rather, our servant. And though he bristles at the notion that anyone should be allowed to instruct his behavior or review his job performance, in November 2010 the voters of America did both.

Realizing this, if I were one of President Obama's advisers, I would've cautioned him greatly on his continued smug and arrogant defiance of the voters, especially as they expressed their thoughts and

183

concerns on the greatest domestic crisis we were facing nationally: the economy.

In mid-April of 2010, when addressing Democratic supporters who paid him (at least his party's campaign fund) between $250 and $1,250 to hear him speak, the president dropped the curtain and let another shade of his true colors show.

In 2009, when the tea parties began forming and the first of what would be more than five thousand of their rallies took place across the nation, he claimed he was barely aware of them, despite the fact that the most watched cable news company reported live from gatherings that ranged from thousands to hundreds of thousands of attendees. (Attendance at these events was a fact about which the White House would directly misguide people throughout 2009.)

But in 2010, instead of playing dumb, the president took a different tactic: arrogance and marginalization. Speaking to people who paid big money to hear him, he said, "I've been a little amused over the last couple of days where people have been having these rallies about taxes. You would think they would be saying, 'thank you.'"[1]

Thank you? For what, exactly, Mr. President?

Since unemployment—which he had pledged to never let grow past 8 percent—had been hovering near 10 percent for the better part of his presidency, should We the People have thanked him for the stimulus bill he passed that drove underemployment rates down even more in dozens of states? He did know, didn't he, that under President Bush nearly one in twenty families worked but did not have enough to make ends meet, but under his administration that percentage had held fairly steady at one in five families?

Or should we have thanked him for the federal takeover of private industry, and the artificial propping up of some companies, while the indiscriminate failures of others went unheeded? Perhaps we could've thanked him for removing the terms "terrorist," "war on terror," and "Islamic radical" from federal usage in any official reference. After all, refusing to label terrorists what they really are would create a more peaceful world . . . right?

Perhaps we could thank him for his repeated attempts through the health care reform bill, his still-not-dead cap-and-trade legislation, and, coming soon, his legislation to normalize illegal aliens. These three alone will put unbearably harsh burdens on the small businesses of America. After all, small businesses only create two of every three new jobs in the nation.

For the president there was also the matter of how he had treated our allies from the moment he had been sworn into office. He treated with contempt our closest ally, Great Britain, and more recently our most important ally in the Middle East, Israel. Yet he gladly shook the hands of dictators, accepted their socialist dogmas as gifts, and even told them that his own nation was a bad player in world affairs. He did so even though if it were not for America, most of the freedoms on the planet presently enjoyed would be relatively nonexistent.

It had become clear to anyone with an ounce of objectivity that he had been and might still be engaged in a great delusion that his own policies were grand and historic. In reality they were substantively, historically, and culturally anti-American, and in some cases significantly dangerous. It is a delusion to think our allies are bad and our enemies are good, but he was so deluded. Worse, he believed it gave him the "right" to arrogantly mock and marginalize those of us who know the truth of the U.S. Constitution: that he works for us.

I wondered, how were we supposed to see "hope and change" in his actions when he mocked us for our needs, priorities, and desires? In reality we'd have preferred him to focus on attempting to heal the sick economy, restore our standing to one of respect among our allies and fear among our enemies, and keep the long reach of government out of our lives. Then we'd have reason to "thank" him! This failure to see the truth had a grossly detrimental effect on a few issues of policy and decision making early on for President Obama. I likened it to a paralysis of sorts, one that would cause him to freeze in place, be incredibly indecisive, and at the end of the day, do too little too late. This paralysis affected his policy and decision making regarding Gitmo, Iraq, Afghanistan, the Iranian uprisings and revolution, the military overthrow in Honduras, and trouble in negotiating with our key allies like Israel.

The paralysis likely caused him a much more effective victory in Afghanistan directly and possibly led to his worst national security decision of his first term.

OBAMA'S GENERAL

When Barack Obama handpicked General Stanley McChrystal to replace the leader in the field operations of the Afghanistan front in the war on terror, he asked McChrystal to issue an assessment early on, to make an official recommendation of a plan of action, and to gauge for him the best-case scenario for the quickest route to bringing troops home.

Months later it was President Obama himself who had left General McChrystal's report sitting stagnant on his desk for the better part of eighteen weeks. In the report the general had drawn plans that focused on one idea: victory over the remaining Taliban forces and al-Qaeda sympathizers.

General McChrystal was the best person President Obama could've picked for the operation. He had been the brains behind the eventual surge victory in Iraq, and though the terrain was significantly different, McChrystal's Afghan strategy was similar in fashion: flood the zone, build rapport, and snuff out the terrorists in the mountain region.

The general had originally requested 80,000 troops for the job. He assured the president that such a troop buildup would bring quick success to the U.S. on the ground. The frozen, deer-in-the-headlights response the president gave to this recommendation communicated a number of things to not only his commander, but to the nation that awaited his decision, and the enemies who are always watching.

Understanding that the president's antiwar supporters would likely never give him the political okay to green-light an 80,000-troop buildup, the general decided to draw up a still-effective strategy that called for half the number of troops—merely 40,000. This concession was a major strategic shift and one to which the president could've easily given the green light.

Instead the administration held nearly a dozen executive, full-cabinet, or partial-cabinet/department head meetings, each lasting several hours. Each time, mysteriously, no decision would be made on McChrystal's recommendations. The action, timeline, and battle plans for the needed coming offensive in Afghanistan would again be delayed.

After all those meetings, dozens upon dozens of hours of discussions, Obama would still not approve the 40,000 troops. Instead he chose to send only 35,000 troops, some of which would not even be ready in time for the offensive. President Obama's inability to make a clear decision for victory in the field had cost several months of preparation, and now he expected the same level of results with fewer than half the troops the general needed.

As a result of Obama's inept and grindingly slow decision making, the enemies felt emboldened, and they went on the offensive. On Obama's watch and at the cost of American soldiers' lives, his administration oversaw fifteen of the bloodiest and costliest (in terms of American lives lost) months of the nearly nine-year-old war.

Soldiers were dying because the president would not make up his mind.

THE WORST ECOLOGICAL
DISASTER IN AMERICAN HISTORY

The 2010 spill in the Gulf had gone on for almost fifty days. Since it began in April, President Obama had had plenty of time to do a great number of things. For example, he attended his second "music party" in less than a week. He was at the Ford's Theatre's "Spirit of America" celebration in Washington. He had also hosted Paul McCartney on the previous Wednesday. The former Beatle serenaded the president's "Michelle" after receiving the Gershwin Prize from the Library of Congress.

During this time BP and the administration were working hand-in-hand to resolve the spill. Yet just the weekend before, British Petroleum's CEO, Tony Hayward, told the BBC that the two men hadn't spoken directly since the rig exploded on April 20, 2010.[2] Even a small business owner like me had to wonder, how can two enormous entities like BP and the government of the United States be genuinely engaged and working together to solve the problem, if one of the two men in question doesn't take the time to pick up the phone and speak to the other? After all, Obama seems to have had time to do plenty of other things.

Senators in the president's own party made the case that the president needed to at least appear to be doing more. They were in the midst of an ugly campaign season, and the administration's inaction seemed to be hurting his party's chances for later that November. A little lesson in crisis management was in order for President Obama, because he seemed to be clueless at the helm of this disaster.

Ecologists and marine biologists were then telling us that the oil spill was causing high toxicity levels in the ocean and along the coastlines, and it was spurring migratory patterns in species living in those waters. Sand/barrier islands would have prevented much of the poison from hitting sensitive marshlands, so why had President Barack Obama denied the requests made by Louisiana and other Gulf states permission to build them? It seemed as though the president was disconnected, and he hadn't found the time to speak to the man he was most dependent upon to get this problem fixed.

Because of my relationship with some of the people involved in the negotiations, I can tell you that BP had expressed frustrations that mirrored those of some of the state leaders in the Gulf. Lots of suggestions and solutions for containment and cleanup of the spill were being put forward, but as of the middle of the summer, the president had only approved funding for roughly one-sixth of the approved solutions.

As the crisis in the Gulf continued, I was all for hearing the normal responses from folks, like "Presidents have to be allowed to multitask." But how could we not insist that President Obama begin by having, at a minimum, one conversation with the man who seemed to be doing the work?

I joked on Fox News at the time, "Hey, I'd even let him use my media company's conference call line if it'd save the tax-payer a buck or two."[3] I also genuinely hoped the burden of all this didn't impact President Obama's goal of not "three putting" this week. You know how unforgiving those angled greens are . . .

And he had played more than forty rounds of golf year to date.

TIME FOR A BIT OF CLARITY

It was still a matter of weeks before the nation was to discover that the president had actually been given knowledge of potential problems with the *Deepwater Horizon* oil rig. In reality his administration had first been alerted in February, nearly six full weeks before the fatal explosion.

But numerous examples have existed in the president's first two years where an inability to make a decision was perhaps as equally costly as if he had made a poor decision, which, in essence, happened twice. In many cases the lengthy time he took to make those decisions caused devastating consequences that were then followed up with even worse decisions.

The obvious lesson here is that ruthless pragmatism leads to a sausage-making decision process. In attempting to curry the favor of everyone, no one is happy. And in the confusion of trying to appease all, the lock on priorities that should override everything else is lost. Presidents shouldn't have trouble making decisions. In the end, it is because of decision-making ability that the people ultimately elect a president. They want him to think clearly and take actions decisively for the welfare of the United States.

It is the least that should be expected.

CHAPTER
TWENTY-ONE

Why Clarity Is Always Superior to Unity

If you get nothing else from the essence of this book, this chapter is the most important one you can read.

Clarity is a lost virtue.

Understanding with crystal-cut precision the important concepts of individual responsibility, risk and reward, and achievement through free and fair competition is not something recent generations have been trained to do well. And liberal/progressive politics are invested in continuing that trend. For by enslaving the masses to the whims of the elite, the elite stay in power. By creating dependency upon the "smart people" the smart people get to make decisions for everyone, and anyone not going along with the prominent thinking of the time is to be viewed as suspect.

Unfortunately, this same pattern has infiltrated not only liberal political action committees and progressive political campaigns, but too often the insulated conservative, Washington-based think-tanks, local churches, and sadly, even our own families.

Therefore it is important to assert regularly that clarity trumps

191

unity . . . always. For demanding unity or unification (more accurate) without demanding an evaluation of the moral foundation on which such unity rests is an assured path to destruction.

The greatest danger in the candidacy of Barack Obama was the willful subverting of substance into an emotional and mushy feeling about "hope" and "change" that was built upon people's fatigue with the struggle against terror, and the immoral action of taking advantage of the troubled economy to bring about a more socialized form of running America.

But if people had thought clearly, regardless of party affiliation, their votes would've been cast differently.

AN IMPORTANT WORD . . .

If Barack Obama, like so many of us, is a product of his environment, upbringing, and influences from childhood forward, then it makes completely understandable sense that he might be confused about what the virtue of genuine clarity looks like.

I was honored to see it modeled in my own life in multiple examples, but none more potent than ones with whom I had constant contact.

WHAT CLARITY LOOKS LIKE

Barack Obama and I have more in common than some may realize. As children, we both struggled to know the men who provided the DNA that created us. Later in life we both had men who were not biologically related to us assume the role of father in our lives. Given that, I would welcome the opportunity to introduce President Obama to two men who greatly impacted my life. Most people just called them Buck and Bob.

Born Norman and James, Buck and Bob were of a different time and era. One began supporting his family at age eight, selling hand-sewn cushions at citywide football games for a few cents per game. He had gotten the idea from watching so many people come to the games and sit in discomfort on the cold cement bleachers in his hometown's football stadium that was used by all of the town's football teams. His entrepreneurial spirit was born of necessity. With older brothers in his life who would not work, and a deceased father, Bob labored even as a child to bring home a few dollars every Friday and Saturday night. By today's standards, it would barely buy a value meal for more than one person, but in his day such effort would help provide groceries or pay an electric bill. At eight years of age on this planet, Bob had figured out that if a man worked hard, using only talents given to him by God, he could use his mind and feed his family.

Likewise, Buck, as a young husband and father, would rise long before dawn. He drove a grocery truck that made stops from early in the morning till late into the evening, and he only got paid for the number of stops he made. It was a very long day—sometimes sixteen to eighteen hours. Buck would report to the warehouse and personally fill his truck with heavy bags of flour, barrels of supplies, and pallets of cans. It was relentless, backbreaking work loading and unloading the truck without help, day in and day out. He did it to feed his family—the ones he loved—so that they could have uninterrupted access to their mom. Without fail, he would rise before sunshine, eat a large breakfast that on some days might be the only meal he had till he was back home that night, and work as hard as any human in America could be asked to. And in the years I've known him, he has never once complained about any of it.

When they were both of the age that was allowed, Bob and Buck served their nation. They were Navy men! And they served in a variety of theaters in what the world would come to know as the costliest global conflict in its history. They both lost friends, saw men die, and survived.

Though they were quite different, they both followed similar paths upon return from the war. Buck, the more bashful one, was able to finally convince his sweetheart to make him breakfast for those early mornings, a task she took to with delight, rising even earlier than he did on most mornings to make by hand homemade biscuits, eggs, bacon, sausage, gravy, fresh fruit, and of course, hot coffee. For the majority of their years on this earth, that routine held, and Buck never allowed her to forget how important that little sign of love was to him.

Upon Bob's return from war, a blushing girl from a big family thought him too much of a charmer to take seriously, but eventually gave in and married the man who never knew a stranger. He was also a man who demonstrated more loyalty to those he loved than anyone who knew him ever realized until long after his death. He eventually had to travel a great deal to keep food on his family's table, but would always point his company car in the direction of home with immediate fervor out of a great desire to see his bride and daughters.

Because of the nature of life in those days, both men had their educations interrupted. Neither of them ever had the chance to darken the doors of Harvard University for even a visit, much less to attend. Buck dropped out of school in only the eighth grade. Bob stopped and started his educational process several times, eventually securing his college degree fairly late in life, by attending night classes, long past the age of any of his contemporaries. Despite their lack of more "obvious" credentials, both Buck and Bob spent their lifetime learning, analyzing, and educating themselves.

Because of this they were fierce competitors, and except on the occasion where they would be pitted against one another, both could regularly be counted on to win whatever game they competed in.

They were both extremely savvy and smart. They were both men of common sense, who had no trouble recognizing God's existence, and who saw to it that their families were in church weekly.

Even though one had a temper of legend, and the other a more passive/aggressive nature, they loved their families.

Each had flaws. Each would easily fess up to mistakes in his life. Each would admit he was but a sinner saved by God's grace.

Buck taught me patience. Bob instilled within me a passion for justice. Buck loved to laugh at the dinner table. Bob would sing in beautiful baritone—especially when he thought no one was listening. Both loved their country and fought for her. Both had moral clarity and could easily define for you the difference between right and wrong.

Both would go out of their way to help their neighbors in need. One would walk a sassy kid back to his mother's doorstep by the earlobe if the situation merited it.

One voted and complained. One shunned talk of politics, but had deep concerns all the same about the direction of the country.

Both were strong in mind and body, both would have given their lives for their families, and both made a bigger contribution to me than I probably can even accurately imagine.

A big piece of me wishes more men—especially our president—could have known them. Perhaps he might not have been so gullibly taken in by the campus communists, socialists, and leftists. Perhaps if Barack had known Buck and Bob, he would have never asserted that America and Islam were one and the same.

I wish that Barack had just had the chance to walk a country road with Buck, or spend an afternoon pulling weeds in the yard with Bob. Perhaps then a love of his country would have taken root in the president's heart, instead of the need to blame her.

Barack will never know Bob, and will most likely never meet Buck.

When it came time to dedicate my second book to someone who embodied the spirit of the kind of man every man should be, Buck and Bob were the only choices in my mind.

America would be a better place if everyone had the opportunity I have had to call them Gramps and Grandpa.

And though I learned much from them, it is my duty to pass on to those who follow all the clarity I can. And on April 25, 2010, I was given that distinct opportunity with the birth of my firstborn son. (I have a previous son from an earlier adoption as well.) Not entirely knowing how to pass it on, I hope the advice I've left will find its way into his heart. But not just his, no, even his entire generation. What follows is a letter I penned for him one day before he was born.

THE NEED TO PASS ON CLARITY

To my first born son,

Within 24-48 hours of the writing of this letter, you sir, will be born. It will be the beginning of your journey. For the first few precious hours, then days, weeks, and months your eyes will pop with excitement at the introduction of any new thing. Yet for all the innocence you will hold for this world around you, sadly, it will do precious little to save any for you. Like every other child, you will have questions. And perhaps for more reasons than most, you will be leveled with expectations. Do not be discouraged by that reality though. Those who expect little or nothing of their lives, more often than not, find it.

Since it is my charge before God to teach and train you, I thought it might be best to explain the way things work in our home. There are a handful of truths you will want to know. For when you operate within them, life for you will be good in every way. Stray from them, son, and you will be in peril. As your father, it is my foremost responsibility to teach you discernment. Deciphering wisdom from every situation in life, by God's grace, I will help you choose the outcome with the best results. Knowing this, please understand that I give you these ideas with the intention of unlocking your potential to radically impact the world you will someday inherit.

1. There IS a God . . .

Though your mother and I will do all we can to give you the fundamental foundation of your faith, there will be mighty forces at work in academia, pop culture, government, and even some claiming to be "Christians" that will attempt to argue this fact. On your college campus, in the first 12 weeks of your freshman year, more than one tenured professor will mock this truth. They will do so to intimidate you into renouncing what is the most important reality of all time. You will not falter, because God will have answered the prayers of your mother and I many times over and you will have living proof as well as historical heritage that God is real, active, and involved in the events of your life.

2. You are responsible for your actions, success, and failures . . .

By the time you turn legal age, the United States may or may not have turned their back on the concept of "individual responsibility." We are in a race against time, and powerful men in the halls of elite places seek to defeat this most American and Biblical of all truths. They are, even as I write to you, penning legislation to allow others to "care for" you because they wish you to believe that you cannot care for yourself. By insuring your dependency upon their "collective" they will have the ability to control most of the choices for your life. They will attempt to rob you of your opportunity at success. Yet in the end, you will come to know this idea more thoroughly than anything else (and mostly because I will repeat it to you beginning the day of your birth), "Your choices will determine your future, and no one else can decide that for you." Because of this reality, you will never be allowed to complain about living life as a victim, even if you are. For history is changed by those who overcome the steepest obstacles, not the ones who succumb to them.

3. Your word is all important . . .

Son, there will be few things you will ever get deeply in trouble for. I know this because your mother and I will simply never allow you, from your earliest stages of life, to set in to place patterns of behavior to empower it in you. From the earliest stages of being able to communicate, you will be expected to tell the truth transparently, and in return, we will always be honest and straight forward with you. Because this will be our agreement, you will come to know early in life that trust is a valuable thing. You will know that there is nothing you cannot be totally honest about with us. And you will know that our love for you will be best evident by giving you sound advice, gut feelings, and honest observations. Honesty, Transparency, and Integrity will be the bare minimum of what you will be expected to contribute to our family, and in return you will have the safest and most joyous place in all the world to call home.

4. Admit faults quickly . . .

No matter how much we may wish you to be the perfect son, we know you will not be. In fact, if parents reap what they've sown as children, then there may be significantly more challenge to you than anything we'd prefer. But that's okay. For we will never expect perfection from you. And in those moments where your actions have disappointed us, and even yourself, if you will tell the truth, come clean quickly, and begin to run the other direction (away from the poor decision), we assure you that you will thrive in life twice as effectively as anyone growing up in your era. Giving an honest and sincere apology is one of the hidden secrets to a life well lived.

5. Clarity trumps unity . . .

My son, there will be many in this world who will attempt to force you into conformity of ideas, behaviors, and principles that will go against the conscience God has given you, and will violate the sense that your mother and I will live out for you. From nearly the day you are born (tomorrow) to the first time you are old enough to read this (and well beyond), the progressives in our world will try to fill your head with lies, half-truths, and deceptions that they hope will cause you to question your beliefs, your God, and your mother and I. From this letter alone they will argue that there is no God, that no one in life can truly be accountable for their own actions, that telling the truth is of little importance, and to never admit when you're wrong. But son, remember that 98% of those in this world who do so will live with tortured souls, haunted by the truths they've ignored, and burdened with the webs upon webs of lies that they are not capable of setting themselves free from. Son, you're not born to be part of the 98%. You've been given this time on earth to be part of the 2% who did it differently, took a stand for what was right, and knew great peace and contentment as a result of doing so.

My son, James Kevin McCullough, born on April 25th 2010, you, sir, are called to know the truth, to live it out, and to encourage others with it. Your decision to seek clarity in life will never go unrewarded, and you could accomplish nothing more in life that would satisfy your mother and I.

After two miscarriages, months of wondering, and 41 weeks of pregnancy we are ready to welcome you into our home.

Our pledge to you is that after eighteen years, we will have poured all we could into you so that you don't merely exist, but genuinely . . . really . . . truly . . . live!

TIME FOR A BIT OF CLARITY

You may be saying to yourself that there isn't a lot about Barack Obama in this particular chapter. I would have to agree but point out the obvious, that there has not been a great deal of clarity emitted from the current administration.

And that's the point. Had President Obama had the honor of sitting at the feet of men deemed great by actions and deeds, character and choices, life and learning, perhaps his own ability to make decisions could have led the United States of America down different roads from what she has seen for the first two years of the Obama presidency.

President Obama in so many ways, while exhibiting all the ruthless pragmatism he can muster, still shows far too often how lost, alone, and without a sense of clear direction his life has endured.

Yet we as Americans have no need to settle for less than absolute clarity. It is what can lead us out of any dark night that our nation may face.

Conclusion

Common Sense, Loyal Opposition: Ultimate Love of Person, Family, and Nation!

THE DEVASTATING SCORECARD

President Obama rode into office on the coattails of some horrible economic realities while promising Americans "hope and change." The nation needed both to energize new policies and to help us continue down the path to recovery, specifically in the areas of job creation and economic growth.

Those who ignorantly—and I use this word literally, not pejoratively—voted for him, have now woken up saying to themselves over and over and over again, "What the heck have I done?"

In 2008, 43 percent of evangelical Christians voted for him, and he rewarded them by turning around and signing an executive order to authorize the spending of millions of dollars for international abortions via the Mexico City policy. And he did it at the peak of the economic meltdown.

Those who wanted America to withdraw from Iraq and to see Gitmo closed are still waiting for those promises to come true.

Afghanistan has seen fifteen of the twenty bloodiest months since our engagement there began while waiting for President Obama to make the decision that he would "follow through" with his decision from March 2010. (And as we came to learn, that was really a reaffirmation of the decision the Bush administration made from the previous November.)

A very interesting side note: the president played more golf in 2009, in the midst of (what pundits began commonly parroting the president's labeling of the economic times) "the worst recession since the Great Depression," than his predecessor played in his entire eight years.

With his cap-and-trade policy the president wants to tax the carbon dioxide produced by everything on the continuum from big and small business to the family pet and farm animal. He also wants to force you to drive a battery-operated car (whose production plants and lithium battery manufacture would create more pollution than all of the oil rigs in the Gulf of Mexico combined.)

On the rest of the domestic front, using whatever tax dollars hadn't already been spent, the president has sought to grab hold of the cash with the broadest expansion of government control in our nation's history through the "reform" of our health care insurance system. He wanted to do this even though numerous polls show at the time an 80+ percent satisfaction rate for Americans with their current health care providers.

Of course, fixing the economy and jobs would've also increased the level of satisfaction with their employer-sponsored health care for even more Americans. (And in the end, fixing the economy and jobs will be his only hope of reelection.)

President Obama accepts awards he is not worthy of (i.e., the Nobel Peace Prize), for things he has not done, and in an interview with Oprah in the summer of 2009, he gave himself a B+ grade on his performance for his first year in office.

So was it any surprise that the Rasmussen daily tracking poll, in what it called the "passion index," began looking at how Americans feel about Mr. Obama's performance and ended up reporting a *record low* on December 13, 2009?[1]

The breakdown went like this (remember, in fewer than twelve months on the job!):

Among *all* the nation's voters: –19%

    Strongly Approve: 23%
    Strongly Disapprove: 42%

Among *only* Democrats:

    Strongly Approve: 41% (so less than half of *just* Democrats)

Among Independents: –28%

    Strongly Approve: 21%
    Strongly Disapprove: 49%

Among those who believe "Economy" is most important issue: –10%

    Strongly Approve: 26%
    Strongly Disapprove: 36%

Among those who believe "Fiscal Policy" is most important issue: –80%

    Strongly Approve: 1%
    Strongly Disapprove: 81%

Change was coming in 2010. For either President Obama would change his policies, or those who have employed him as our administrator in chief would dismiss many of his allies in Congress (as they did in resounding ways) and serve him notice that his job performance was poor in the mid-course review period.

He's our employee. We should never allow him or any other elected official to forget that central truth.

TIME FOR A BIT OF CAUTION

If in reading this material, especially in the early portion of 2011 or 2012, you believe that the narrative I've laid out here is so devastating that reelection is an entirely impossible scenario, let me strongly encourage you to think otherwise.

The midterms served up a "shellacking," in his own words, that the president will not soon forget.[2] But he is not the first to suffer this embarrassment. In 1994, then president Bill Clinton was served similar notice. He used the lessons of that midterm election to begin to postulate to greater precision his political tool of triangulation. On policy after policy he peeled away enough credit from Congress to win an overwhelming reelection against the not-very-formidable opponent, Bob Dole.

Many have second-guessed what President Obama's choices are and where he goes from the outbreak of the record-setting midterm losses. I can only state what I would advise him to do. Here are ten places where he should start:

1. He should begin to make peace with the Tea Party and abandon the roots of the socialist and Marxist influences in his life. The beliefs they hold are anti-American. They are anti-freedom. They are anti–individual responsibility. And they are anti-risk/reward.
2. He should somehow square his claims of faith with his anti-faith practices: abortion, the redefinition of marriage, the persistent and inexplicably ineffective defense of embryonic stem-cell research, the revoking of doctors' conscience rights, the subjection of clergy to perform commitment ceremonies in morally questionable circumstances, the insistence on the sexual radicalization of the military, and many, many, more.

3. He should allow the American people to see him change his own hostile positions against small business, and he should do much more to encourage the development of small business, small business growth, and small business expansion.

4. He should begin to call our enemies what they are: terrorists, murderous dogs who seek to destroy America for what she is, a beacon of hope to anyone who is seeking.

5. He should publicly and loudly petition Congress for a fairly large increase and a greater efficiency of the legal immigration process. He should demand the expansion of legal immigration, hold town meetings, make commercials of crying mothers, and challenge those in agreement to rise up.

6. He should also build a southern border barrier that is impenetrable and demand employer accountability for hiring people who were illegal, and he should congratulate states that have the courage to deal with the problems associated with these issues, instead of scolding them for doing so.

7. He should seek to eliminate or greatly reduce the tax burdens on the job-creating sectors of society and do away with the estate tax and marriage tax penalties—forever.

8. He should demand that America be listened to in the global conversation of how to fight global terrorism, and he should see to it that nations know that anyone who harbors terror operations will be seen as terrorists themselves.

9. He should ask for the American people's prayers.

10. He should find a way to express genuine faith, hope, and encouragement to the people he serves.

The questions before us, not just for the remainder of the Obama administration but for the administrations to follow it, are simple. Will we continue to be prosperous? Will we be a nation known for principles? And will we pass these down to the generations we leave behind?

As then candidate Obama repeatedly ginned up emotional reaction on the campaign trail of 2008, he made repeated promises of things that he would accomplish. The results have all fallen short. But this is not an indication of his final effectiveness. And those who are opposed to his principles should be aware of this reality and remain engaged in the process because of it.

America only works best if the debate over ideas is constant.

The Scripture talks about the concept of iron sharpening iron (Proverbs 27:17). It never says a tree branch sharpens iron . . . because it can't. And neither will "sharpening" occur in this country if the debate of ideas, the factory of suggestions, the birth of renovation, and the conceptualization of solutions ever becomes one-sided.

For the first two full years of the Obama administration, his influence has been felt in nearly every level of American life. And for many, we've decided that is simply too much influence. But now, friend, great opportunity sits at our doorstep and wonders at what our reaction will be. Will we drive through the obstacles in front of us, or will we succumb to the idea that we should let the "smart" people handle them?

Will we sit and discuss the future of our hopes while allowing the best opportunity to achieve them pass us by on the road, or will we think clearly?

Are we willing to challenge ourselves to refine our ability to think, to process, to weigh, to determine, and to decide, or will we let it become rusty? Or even worse, especially from a moral standpoint, will we allow it to become ruthless and pragmatic? Will we then believe?

When those who oppose, who criticize, who put down, who shout loud in an attempt to intimidate us out of our belief system, not on substance but on sheer emotion and anger, will we hold fast knowing that our beliefs have been born out of sound thought?

Will we then act?

Will we when necessary loyally oppose the forces that seek to undermine the definitions of faith, freedom, family, or America? Will we, in instances both great and small, stand, march, speak, and inspire? Will we choose action over hopelessness? Will we choose behavior over intimidation? Will we choose engagement over argument?

Then what shall be our impact?

We must think on things that are true! Admittedly, this can be a challenging way to live. Daily attempting to process and understand life is tiring and requires the sacrifice of time, but what are the options? Do we wish to die as vegetables, well fed on television?

If we love our fellow man, we will strive to encourage him to think with clarity as well. If we love our neighbor as ourselves, we will seek paths to encourage self-reliance instead of government dependency. If we cherish our six-month-old baby, we will whisper in his ear, "The world I leave for you will be better for the fights I've waged to protect you from."

All in all, friend, it's a simple reality. Choose to think with clarity . . . and your reputation will allow you to rise above those who seek to level the outcomes. Choose to believe with clarity, and your reputation will allow you the purity of a clean conscience.

Choose to act with clarity, and the confidence you have in your own behavior will be reflected in those nearest you in terms of trust.

Choose to have an impact of clarity, and when the leader of the free world seeks to enslave the masses by having them recite a mantra that is far more emotion than substance, "Yes, We Can," you will be able to stop his entire universe. You will draw a line between you and him, place your foot on the chalk, and say with determination and confidence, "No, you can't!"

God be with you as you stand!

Notes

CHAPTER 1

1. Byron York, "Spill reveals Obama's lack of Executive Experience," *Washington Examiner*, June 8, 2010, http://washingtonexaminer.com/politics/spill-reveals-obama039s-lack-executive-experience.
2. "Obama Is Going to Pay for My Gas and Mortgage!!!" http://www.youtube.com/watch?v=P36x8rTb3jI, posted by user ChiTraderRob.
3. Barack Obama at an Obama for President campaign stop, Kansas City, MO, 2008.
4. Barack Obama, "State of the Union Address 2010 (Full Text): Read Obama's Speech," *Huffington Post*, January 27, 2010, http://www.huffingtonpost.com/2010/01/27/state-of-the-union-2010-full-text-transcript_n_439459.html.
5. Charles Hurt in DC and David Seifman and Jennifer Fermino in NY, "Dem Health Rx a Poison Pill in NY: Terrifying 57% Tax Looms for Biggest Earners, *New York Post*, July 16, 2009, http://www.nypost.com/p/news/regional/item_3AApff75KCb9ZbMkjSC8PO. Used by permission of *New York Post*.

CHAPTER 2

1. Barack Obama, Remarks by the President in State of the Union Address, White House, Office of the Defense Secretary,

January 27, 2010, http://www.whitehouse.gov/the-press-office/
remarks-president-state-union-address.

2. http://cdn.iextract.quadrat4.de/images/35fe953ca1f839d6da0df74aec6d
6bd2.jpg.

3. Rasmussen Daily Tracking poll, March 15, 2009.

4. "Video Killed the Radio Star," written by Geoff Downes, Trevor Horn,
and Bruce Woolley, from the Buggles' album *The Age of Plastic* (1979).

CHAPTER 3

1. "Melissa Etheridge Refuses to Pay Taxes over Gay-Marriage Ban," *TV
Guide*, November 8, 2008.

2. "Obama's Second Primetime Press Conference," *Huffington Post*, March
24, 2009, http://www.huffingtonpost.com/2009/03/24/obamas-second-
primetime-p_n_178794.html.

CHAPTER 4

1. Paul Steinhauser, "Obama and GOP disagree on May job numbers," CNN
Politics Political Ticker (blog), June 4, 2010, http://politicalticker.blogs
.cnn.com/2010/06/04/obama-and-gop-disagree-on-may-job-numbers/.

2. Zennie62, "U.S. Unemployment and Underemployment Rate at 17
Percent," *San Francisco Chronicle*, January 19, 2010, http://www.sfgate
.com/cgi-bin/blogs/abraham/detail?entry_id=55573.

3. http://www.whitehouse.gov/blog/Facts-Are-Stubborn-Things/.

4. Short aside: To a lesser degree but still of importance, our neighbors to
the north had gone into a recession roughly the same time we did. They
did bite their lip and grind it out. They did not infuse their economy
with large amounts of funny money or stimulus dollars. Instead they
decentralized some aspects of Canadian life and along with many of
our allies in the West, headed in a philosophical and practical direction
that seemed to indicate that these nations believed economies were best
fixed in private hands, not on the government dole. It should be noted
that in less than eighteen months, Canada's economy had more than
recovered fully and was creating jobs at a faster clip than what the Obama
administration was able to claim eighteen months into their "recovery"
program.

5. http://www.america.gov/st/usg-english/2008/November/20081105101958 abretnuh0.580044.html.
6. http://hotair.com/archives/2009/white-house-using-base-closure-process-to-extort-nelsons-vote-on-obamacare/

CHAPTER 6

1. Rush Limbaugh, "I Hope Obama Fails," *The Rush Limbaugh Show* (transcript), January 16, 2009, http://www.rushlimbaugh.com/home/daily/site_011609/content/01125113.guest.html.
2. Obama: Crisis Is a Time of "Great Opportunity" (VIDEO), *Huffington Post* (online), March 7, 2009, http://www.huffingtonpost.com/2009/03/07/obama-crisis-is-a-time-of_n_172731.html.
3. Tim Graham, "Rachel Maddox on Leno: Limbaugh Should Back Socialism Once It's Enacted," NewsBusters, March 5, 2009, http://newsbusters.org/blogs/tim-graham/2009/03/05/rachel-maddow-leno-limbaugh-should-back-socialism-once-its-enacted.
4. Kevin McCullough, "Why the Obama Administration Will Implode in Weeks," Fox News, September 1, 2009, http://www.foxnews.com/opinion/2009/09/01/kevin-mccullough-obama-implode/#.
5. Ibid.
6. Ibid.
7. Barack Obama, "Obama: My Plan Makes Electricity Rates Skyrocket" (video), YouTube, http://www.youtube.com/watch?v=HlTxGHn4sH4, posted by user BattleBornPAC, March 18, 2009.
8. Excerpted from the Leonard Shapiro story that appeared on page A1 of the *Washington Post*, Thursday, October 2, 2003. Last known link to the story: http://www.washingtonpost.com/wp-dyn/articles/A34359-2003Oct2.html.

CHAPTER 7

1. Barack Obama, "Obama's Victory Speech" (transcript), posted on *New York Times* Election Results 2008 page, November 5, 2008, http://elections.nytimes.com/2008/results/president/speeches/obama-victory-speech.html, emphasis added.
2. Barack Obama, "Obama Cracks Jokes on Leno Show, Makes 'Special Olympics' Gaffe," Daniel Kurtzman's Political Humor Blog on About

.com, March 20, 2009, http://politicalhumor.about.com/b/2009/03/20/
obama-cracks-jokes-on-leno-show-rolls-gutter-ball.htm.
3. Julie A. Seymour, "CNBC's Kernen: 'You Might Not Have Fixed Global
Warming' After D-Day: 'Oracle of Omaha' Warren Buffett agrees, says job
1, 2 and 3 must be the 'economic war,'" Media Research Institute Web site,
March 9, 2009, http://www.mrc.org/bmi/articles/2009/CNBCs_Kernen_
You_Might_Not_Have_Fixed_Global_Warming_After_DDay.html.
4. "Obama Call for 'International Order' Raises Questions About U.S.
Sovereignty," FoxNews.com, May 24, 2010, http://www.foxnews.com/
politics/2010/05/24/obama-international-order-raises-questions-
sovereignty/.
5. Lisa Mascaro and Christi Parsons, "Obama Calls for a Strategy of Global
Cooperation," *Los Angeles Times*, May 23, 2010, http://articles.latimes
.com/2010/may/23/nation/la-na-obama-west-point-20100523.

CHAPTER 8

1. Kevin McCullough, "Chavez to Obama, 'Happy 4th. Now stick 'em up,'"
Townhall.com, http://townhall.com/columnists/KevinMcCullough/
2010/07/04/chavez_to_obama,_happy_4th_now_stick_em_up/page/full/.
2. Kevin McCullough, "Welcome to the Terrorists-for-Jobs Exchange,"
FoxNews.com, November 16, 2009, http://www.foxnews.com/
opinion/2009/11/16/kevin-mccullough-terrorists-prisons-jobs/.
3. *Illinois Job Index, MSA Report, Illinois Coalition for Jobs Growth &
Prosperity*, released June 2006, http://www.real.illinois.edu/IEO/MSA_
JobIndex06/june2006ilmsajobindex.pdf.
4. "Obama remarks during Iftar dinner at The White House" (speech
transcript), *Washington Post*, August 13, 2010, http://projects
.washingtonpost.com/obama-speeches/speech/364/.

CHAPTER 10

1. "'One in four' of U.S. Muslims under 30 'say suicide bombings to defend
their religion are acceptable at least in some circumstances,'" Jihad Watch,
http://www.jihadwatch.org/2007/05/one-in-four-of-us-muslims-under-30-
say-suicide-bombings-to-defend-their-religion-are-acceptable-at-l.html.
2. Ibid.

CHAPTER 11

1. Anne E. Kornblut, "Obama reviews Christmas Day plane attack in radio address," 44: Politics, *Washington Post*, January 2, 2010, http://voices .washingtonpost.com/44/2010/01/obama-reviews-christmas-day-pl .html?nav=rss_email/components.

CHAPTER 12

1. (http://www.guardian.co.uk/world/2010/mar/01/barack-obama-told-to-quit-smoking)

CHAPTER 13

1. http://www.academia.org/queering-elementary-education/.

CHAPTER 14

1. http://www.realclearpolitics.com/video/2009/07/22/obama_doctors_taking _tonsils_out_for_money_instead_of_diagnosing_it_as_allergies.html.
2. http://www.youtube.com/watch?v=SG56B2et4M8.
3. Meredith Jessup, "Euthanasia? You Decide: Obama in His Own Words," The Tipsheet, Townhall.com, http://townhall.com/tipsheet/ MeredithJessup/2009/08/12/euthanasia_you_decide_obama_in_his_ own_words.

CHAPTER 16

1. James Crowley, "Obama: Police who arrested professor 'acted stupidly,'" July 22, 2009, *CNN*, http://articles.cnn.com/2009-07-22/us/harvard.gates .interview_1_cambridge-police-gates-james-crowley?_s=PM:US.
2. Joseph Williams, "Obama scolds Cambridge police: President, a friend of Gates, says officers 'acted stupidly,'" *Boston Globe*, July 23, 2009,

http://www.boston.com/news/nation/washington/articles/2009/07/23/
obama_scolds_cambridge_police/.

3. Brian Ross and Rehab El Buri, "Obama's Pastor: God Damn America,
U.S. to Blame for 9/11," ABCNews, Blotter, March 13, 2008, http://
abcnews.go.com/Botter/story?id=4443788.

4. A reference to Matthew 25:40 from the King James Version of the Bible.

CHAPTER 17

1. Kevin McCullough, "Why Obama Sycophants Are So Compromised,"
RochesterConservative.com, September 28, 2009, http://www
.rochesterconservative.com/blog/why-obama-sycophants-
are-so-compromised/.

2. See "YouTube—Elementary School Children Praises Obama," http://
www.youtube.com/watch?v=Iv8Rl3QBwMc.

3. McCullough, "Why Obama Sycophants Are So Compromised."

4. Kevin McCullough, "Banned: The American Flag on Cinco de Mayo,"
Townhall.com, http://townhall.com/columnists/KevinMcCullough/
2010/05/09/banned_the_american_flag_on_cinco_de_mayo/page/full/.

CHAPTER 18

1. "A Massive and Potentially Unprecedented Disaster," White House
Blog, posted by Jesse Lee on May 2, 2010, http://www.whitehouse
.gov/blog/2010/05/02/a-massive-and-potentially-unprecedented-
environmental-disaster.

2. Marisa Taylor, "Since spill, feds have given 27 waivers to oil companies in
gulf," Sun-Herald.com (Biloxi, Gulfport, and south Mississippi), May 9,
2010, http://www.sunherald.com/2010/05/07/2164885/since-spill-feds-
have-given-27.html.

3. Ibid.

CHAPTER 19

1. Kevin McCullough, "On Sestak v. White House: Crime isn't the only
issue," May 30, 2010, Townhall.com, http://townhall.com/columnists/

KevinMcCullough/2010/05/30/on_sestak_v_white_house_crime_
isnt_the_only_issue.
2. ˙ See http://codes.lp.findlaw.com/uscode/18/I/29/600.
3. McCullough, "On Sestak v. White House," http://www.freerepublic.com/
focus/f-news/2524158/posts.

CHAPTER 20

1. Dominique Pastre, contrib., "Obama Renews Call for Bipartisanship,
Takes Jab at Tea Partiers," April 16, 2010, Fox News, http://www.foxnews
.com/politics/2010/04/15/
obama-renews-bipartisanship-takes-jab-tea-partiers/.
2. Bryan Lysaght, "BP's CEO Hasn't Spoken Directly with Obama About
Leak (Update 1)," Bloomberg.com, June 6, 2010, http://www.bloomberg
.com/apps/news?pid=newsarchive&sid=asQDvBNvDFIE.
3. Kevin McCullough, "Hey, Mr. President, Pick Up the Dang Phone!"
FoxNews.com, June 7, 2010, http://forums.corvetteforum.com/
politics-religion-and-controversy/2611823-obama-hasnt-talked-to-bp-
ceo-since-april-20th.html.

CONCLUSION

1. http://www.rasmussenreports.com/public_content/politics/
obama_administration/daily_presidential_tracking_poll.
2. See Associated Press, "Obama spares turkeys 'shellacking' he got at
polls," November 24, 2010, MSNBC.com, http://www.msnbc.msn.com/
id/40355379/ns/politics-more_politics/.

About the Author

Kevin McCullough is a nationally syndicated radio talk show host and columnist who tackles news and current events from a Christian perspective. As the author of *MuscleHead Revolution* and *The Kind of Man Every Man Should Be*, his approach to politics and values has garnered a large following of loyal listeners and readers.

Acknowledgments

My Savior: for Jesus is the first and last!

My lovely bride, for all that she does to make me a better man, husband, father, and thinker . . . every single day!

The entire crew at Thomas Nelson: Joel, Kristen, and Renee, your encouragement kept me going and made me a better writer!

Jonathan Garthwaite at Townhall.com, for letting me paint crazy all over his editorial pages every Sunday.

Lynne Jordal Martin of Fox News, who is the best opinion editor anyone will ever have the honor of working with!

Dr. Ray Pritchard for reminding me that writing actually begins by verbally throwing up all over the page.

Stephen Baldwin, my brother from another mother.

Ivan, Kerri, Jacqueline, and Baby Karl, the posse that keeps the XtreMEDIA trains running.

Jonathan Clements, who in great faith envisioned this day before I did.

And finally to the listeners on all 289 radio stations who hear me weekly and the viewers in all 30.2 million households who watch, for their desire to become "Binge Thinkers" and for their courage to see life as it is, not as some would like us to see it.